A WOMAN OF GOLD

A Biography of Family, Faith, and Business

Robert W. Killick, PhD

Balboa Press books may be ordered through booksellers or by contacting:

Balboa Press
A Division of Hay House
1663 Liberty Drive
Bloomington, IN 47403
www.balboapress.com.au
AU TFN: 1 800 844 925 (Toll Free inside Australia)
AU Local: (02) 8310 7086 (+61 2 8310 7086 from outside Australia)

Print information available on the last page.

ISBN: 978-1-9822-9969-9 (sc)
ISBN: 978-1-9822-9970-5 (hc)
ISBN: 978-1-9822-9968-2 (e)

Library of Congress Control Number: 2024910046

Balboa Press rev. date: 06/14/2024

We acknowledge Fairfax Syndication for the use of the article that appeared in the *The Age,* Saturday, September 13, 2003.

For Judy with all thanks for sixty-four fantastic years as the front lady of the Punch and Judy Travelling Show as well as roles including the Beautiful Lady Alice, Cora, Gracie, and Mabel. It has been wonderful that together we have discovered that thanksgiving is the dialect of heaven.

Our Lord lets things grow until they're perfect.
- Anonymous

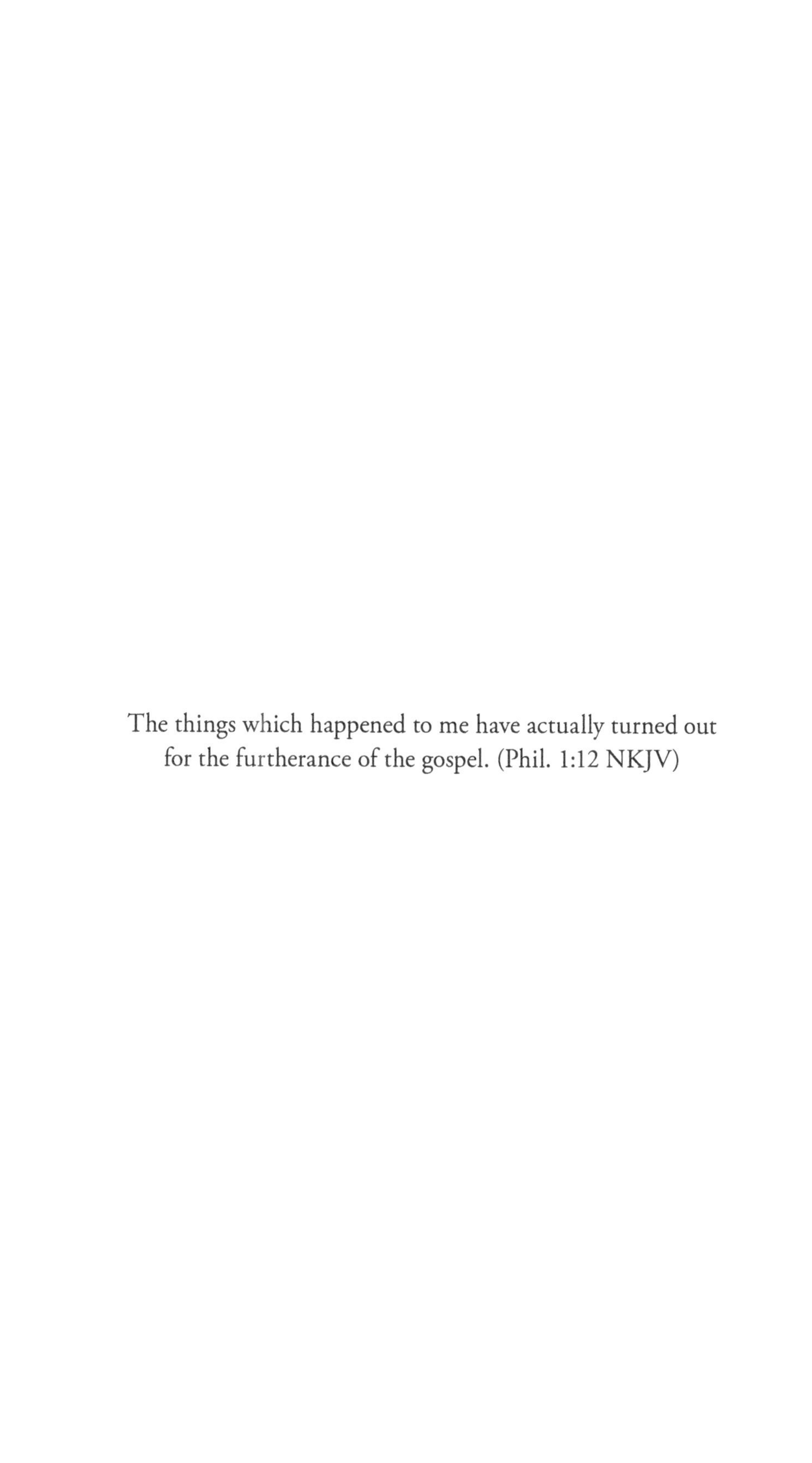

The things which happened to me have actually turned out for the furtherance of the gospel. (Phil. 1:12 NKJV)

CONTENTS

SOME THOUGHTS ABOUT THE AUTHOR

Even after sixty-three years of marriage, my friends tell me I am brave to write my wife's biography.

However, I have always worked on the principle that "fortune favours the brave." But anyway, what can go wrong? I mean, I don't forget her birthday and where she was born! I know the story of how she went back to night school so she could reach the level of education to become a primary schoolteacher. I know of her achievements and the work she has done. I also have a feel to understanding how she has become a person of significance through business, her family, and her ministries in the church and in her social milieu. Nevertheless, we shall not forget Shakespeare's well-remembered prayer put on the lips of Hamlet's guards: "Angels and ministers of grace, defend us."

Hagar

Truth in comic form.

But yes, I will be brave, which Judy told me to be! I have inveigled David Oliver, one of my esteemed friends, to provide some insights into me and the Punch and Judy Travelling Show.

David writes:

"Merely corroborative detail, intended to give artistic verisimilitude to an otherwise bald and unconvincing narrative." (*The Mikado*)

No, not at all. Indeed, what follows is the truth and nothing but the truth!

I have known of Dr Robert (Bob) Killick and his wife, Judy, and their family for around thirty-five years, but it has only been in the last ten to fifteen years or so that I have become much more aware of and so much more appreciative of Bob and Judy. We've become good friends, even true confidantes.

I have always admired Bob, but actually, at first I was a little hesitant to speak in certain situations like meetings of our Syndal Church Diaconate and later the Church council as this man was and is known for his outstanding leadership, business acumen, and in all humility, is a true Christian gentleman, husband, father, and friend. He's never claimed that; it is what people say of him.

He lives in a way that always asks, "Why not?" rather than "Why?" And he leads by example in both words and actions. He has a wonderful memory for God's Word, an ability to use those words to encourage and acknowledge others, and is not afraid to jump in and do what needs to be done.

I have grown to love his ability to find just the right scripture—from memory—for any conversation we are engaged in, and his general knowledge and intellect are awesome. He is also very well-read and enjoys the theatre, especially quoting Gilbert and Sullivan, hence my opening line from *The Mikado*.

After scripture verses, "The show must go on" is perhaps Bob's favourite saying and for good reason. Alongside the more serious aspects and responsibilities of life, Bob and Judy have been able to incorporate their talents, skills, and entrepreneurship to bring fun and music to many opportunities, especially their birthdays and celebrations to which everyone is invited. This has been a lifelong habit and gift, and thousands of family, friends, and visitors have enjoyed the concerts and parties. What is a concert if you don't have at least three hundred close friends present?

Bob—and Judy—are wonderful Christian people, giving themselves to God's Word and work as a priority, and living out Philippians 4:8 every day in ways that go way beyond caring and includes unbelievable generosity.

I have the honour these days of working alongside Bob and Judy to assist in their business and personal responsibilities, so we meet two or three times a week and chat on the phone almost every day. Bob continues to be the humble, caring, and generous person I have known for thirty-five years. In his business, he is a friend to his employees and colleagues and greatly respected around the world where he has established his company name and services. To his family, he is a loving, devoted, and generous father, grandfather, and great-grandfather. And to his friends—and he counts everyone as a friend—he is loyal and dependable. As a Christian, Bob embodies the attributes given in God's Word, and I know him to be an extraordinary example and role model.

My wife, Elaine, and I are indeed grateful to have been asked to provide these comments on Bob.

Finally, brothers, whatever is true, whatever is honourable, whatever is just, whatever is pure, whatever is lovely, whatever is commendable, if there is any excellence, if there is anything worthy of praise, think about these things. (Phil. 4:8)

From an Educational Perspective

The following biography provides the story of what has taken baby Judy into her eighties, and to quote the old song, "You must have been a beautiful baby, for baby look at you now!" As there might be those reading who have never met Judy "in the flesh," what follows is the briefest sketch of "that girl." It has been prepared by a close friend, Mrs Judy Enticott, a former teacher and later an administrator of a community education program.

> "Blessed to be a blessing," the Killick family motto, truly describes Judy's life as she embraces God's gifts and in turn showers blessings on a countless number of people with whom she comes into contact, be they family, friends, church, or casual acquaintances.
>
> Judy has a rare and precious gift because she can, on the one hand, be the life of the party, whose approach to life is uplifting and energizing. She can be full of fun, lifting spirits and leaving an audience in awe and admiration at her agility, numerous talents, and bubbling enthusiasm for life. In her piano playing, stage performances, and animated conversations, the observer is sometimes left breathless. She has charisma, a beautiful voice, and twinkling eyes that communicate mischief and fun. She simply makes you feel better for having spent time with her.
>
> On the other hand, Judy demonstrates the God-given gift of genuine empathetic listening and wise counsel. God's love radiates through her whole being. Judy has the ability to engage those around her in conversation so that they feel a real sense of belonging, of being part of a community.
>
> Judy draws people into her life, and her home is always open and inviting. Her garden provides the beautiful roses and daphne that become posies to give to those she visits. Her kitchen is always welcoming with a seat that captures the streaming sun and with a cuppa at the ready. This is how home should be. It is a place where each person feels like an honoured guest. In the words Judy says, the listener knows to expect to hear God's wisdom, beautifully expressed, with scripture quotes sprinkling

the conversation in a most natural way. In Judy's attitude, you feel God's love and concern and know that she will intercede in prayer long after the conversation has ended.

I believe Syndal Baptist Church was very wise in its appointment of Judy as an elder many years ago because God's wisdom is evident in all her words and actions. I am encouraged by her constant reminder to "Keep looking up," which has provided great peace and reassurance, helping me to focus on Jesus in good and difficult periods of life.

When health issues prevented Judy from driving for a period, she didn't stop, she simply learnt to ride an electric bike so that she could continue to visit the sick. That, quite simply, amazed me. Many others would have stopped, but Judy persevered so that she could continue to encourage the housebound. I was greatly inspired during this period by Judy's acknowledgement that everything was in God's plan and was not at all surprised when, after several months, Judy was invited to sit the required tests that led to her being able to resume driving.

I thank God for Judy's influence in my life, for her consistent encouragement, and her nonjudgmental attitude. I thank her for the many reminders of God's love and protection and feel truly blessed to be able to call her "friend."

From a teenager's perspective

On our first Sunday at Port Sunlight, near Birkenhead, England, the Lord guided us to walk to the local New Ferry Methodist Church. It was there that we met Cyril Harvey, a sergeant of police, Hilda, his wife, and their twin daughters, Pam and Katey, who were then aged fifteen. Sixty years later, Pam has recalled those days of yore:

My first recollection of Judy has stayed with me. We had just finished a service at church and were about to drive home with our parents. All of a sudden, a lady dressed in a navy-blue coat and a charming small hat ran—darted is actually more like it—across the road as if she had something urgent to tell our parents. She was laughing and talking, a bundle of energy, smiling as she spoke and radiating warmth. I was captivated by her lovely Australian accent (which sounded melodic to my young ears), and by her energy. English folk weren't too exuberant in those days, probably still reeling from six years of a terrible war, but Judy sure was. When she left the car, again running back across the road, I remember my mother saying, "Isn't she lovely?" Oh yes, she was and still is.

We remained friends during Bob and Judy's stay in England and beyond, my parents "adopting" them as their own. They were enriched by Bob and Judy's faith, their openness about their faith, and the new life they stirred within the church, especially through the prayer group.

I remember Judy as a wonderful mother to Jenni and later Andrew, who was born in England. Motherhood was yet another aspect of her character that was lovely to observe at close hand. And I know that my mother, who was a "mother" to everyone she met, cherished being around this young family with a toddler and baby.

I was certainly entranced by them. Judy would constantly laugh at Bob's antics, like throwing hot water on an icy car windshield in the winter. To us staid British, this was a breath of fresh air! Everything seemed to be fun to Judy. She took everything in her stride, and to me, she seemed to be the embodiment of someone who was at peace, who walked with her faith each day while sharing her happiness and joy with everyone she met. She was approachable and intelligent, steadfast, and firm in her faith; her warmth and humour captured my heart. In truth, I'd never met anyone quite like Judy.

As a teenager on the cusp of womanhood, searching for answers to my many unanswered questions about religion and life in general, Judy subconsciously became a wonderful role model to my adolescent mind. She enabled me to see that it was just fine to ask questions, how to be at ease using warmth and wit, and that it was acceptable to think for myself and form my own opinions. And she did this with her unwavering jocularity, intelligence, and absolute joy of life!

Looking back now over sixty years, I am extremely grateful to Judy for her friendship and love in those early days and for her ongoing friendship and warmth over the years. I know with certainty that I'm a better person because of her; she taught me a great deal without even knowing or trying. And it's beautiful to know that she's still that lovely, laughing, smiling, intelligent, and warm woman she always was, one who has never ceased to love her Lord as a most faithful and loyal servant.

May God continue to bless her each and every day.

FOREWORD

From a Societal Perspective

Small in stature and not taking up much space but in terms of influence and impact, Judy Killick is a woman whose life has made a significant difference to many, not the least of whom are her family. *Woman of Gold* is a fitting title for a book that shares the story of Judy Killick, whom I have had the privilege of knowing and calling a friend for over fifty-two years.

Judy exudes enthusiasm and loves to engage with people. Along with her husband, Bob, Judy has extended hospitality and a welcome to hundreds of people in their home. Judy has often been described as the life of a party, and it is true! Again, with Bob, she is also often hosting parties.

Judy has a vibrant faith in Jesus and a passion to help as many people as possible to know about and to know Jesus. As well, she has a great commitment to ensuring that people know that they are cared for and loved. Her untiring efforts to pastorally support and encourage people have seen her phoning, visiting, praying for, and practically helping scores of people. Her generosity of time, energy, and resources have been great gifts to others, and she stewards these resources very well. Over the years, Judy's seemingly boundless energy and care have encouraged people to deal with challenges, have hope, move forward, and have a go at things.

Judy Killick's life has been full of adventure and invested in causes that are much bigger than she is. She is a woman of gold, and her story will inspire and challenge.

I recommend this book to you.

Bill Brown, BScEd, BD, DMin
Emeritus Pastor, Syndal Baptist Church, Melbourne, Australia

PREFACE

Use of Editorials

Stored in the archives of the Syndal Baptist Church are the weekly newsletters that are disseminated each Sunday. On the cover is an article to provide weekly encouragements, exhortations, some theology, a rallying cry, and even a pep talk. These are generically known as "the Editorials." During the author's times as the church secretary (lay leader), it became the custom to write the weekly editorial. The main periods of these writings were 1984–1985 and 1991–1992. Where these touch on something apposite in Judy's life, one or several Editorials have been added to the biography.

Some of the links may be considered tenuous, but just put it down to the author's quirky mind and Judy's encouragement for their inclusion in the text. For example, the link to the "A Blank Sheet" Editorial below lies in that when I started to write Judy's biography a few hours ago, I started with a blank sheet. OK, OK, these days, it is a blank computer screen. As much as possible, the Editorials have been left unchanged from the originals.

Vol. 34, No. 11, Sunday, 17 March 1991

A Blank Sheet (1)

There is something formidable to look at a blank sheet of paper and know an editorial has to be written.

I was chatting the other day and commented that the best of life was yet to come! I was told that from where this person was coming, they did not believe it.

Today is a ***blank*** sheet on which we write *if* we neither carry in the failures of the past nor bring in the fear of the future. Paul reminds us, "to forget what lies behind" (Phil. 3:13), and Jesus tells us not to fear the future being of such value to God (Matt. 10:26–31).

OK, I hear you saying, "You still don't know my situation." No, I don't, but God does! He is the one that calls us not to just forget what lies behind, but to strain to reach the prize for which He is calling us up to heaven (Phil. 3:14).

Yes, this blank sheet is filling fast, but then it is on to the rest of the day. Let's chase each day with a life that is pleasing to God (1 Thess. 4:1).

Bob Killick

PS—On your marks, get set …

....

Vol. 34, No. 12, Sunday, 24 March 1991

A Blank Sheet (2)

The other Sunday I fleetingly shook the hand of a good friend as our paths crossed in our church's crowded fellowship area after the 11 a.m. service. When I returned a week later from business in Sydney, I heard that Brian had died on the Monday morning following our brief salutations. It gave me more than a pause to think. Was there anything else I could, or should, have said? But then we don't really know in God's providence how long each one of us has to live. We certainly assume we have forever.

My mind then began to meditate further around that blank sheet of paper, which we touched on last week as a symbol of each day of our lives. There is something very fragile about a sheet of paper.

The Bible uses two other images warning us on the fragility of life. The first describes our impact as but a mist that appears for a short time and then vanishes (James 4:14).

The second is when God sees us frail tents that can be pulled down at any time (2 Cor. 5:1–4). It is similar to a blank sheet of paper, which can be folded up by the Lord and put in His pocket.

There is the apocryphal story of many years ago telling of a ship berthing from Africa at New York. It carried President Theodore Roosevelt returning from big game hunting and an old couple who had spent a hard life in missionary endeavour. They went unnoticed in the thronging crowd who cheered the president on his way back to the White House. During the evening at a hotel, the couple mused on why there had been no greetings after their hard but mostly successful work. But then came the assurance from the Lord: "But you are not *home* yet!"

Oh, to be home with the Lord (Phi. 1:23; John 14:1–3).

Bob Killick

PS: One day …

....

Vol. 34, No. 13, Sunday, 31 March 1991

A Blank Sheet (3)

For people of my generation and older, the idea of a blank sheet of paper is really rather quaint. I mean at school, I was brought up with ink, which seemed to have a predilection to smudge the cleanest blank sheet.

On the day we call Good Friday, we remember that on the blank sheet of history, black ink was read over that day for "at noon the whole country was covered with darkness, which lasted for three hours" (Matt. 27:45). It was the hour of evil triumphant!

From the books of C. S. Lewis to Tony Campolo, we can read their fictional descriptions of the exultation of Satan and his cohorts as Christ died on the cross. Without much imagination added to the Bible, we can think of the satisfaction of the Pharisees on the elimination of the troublemaker (John 11:47–50) to Pilate who had solved the riddle of truth (John 18:38) to the feckless crowd (Matt. 21:9; 27:22).

Yes, it was Friday, and the ink was right across the sheet.

But Sunday was coming!

We sometimes feel that all is black, there is no hope, but then Sunday is yet to be.

If Christ has not risen, we are of all of people most miserable (1 Cor. 15:19–20); but *He has risen!* The ink stains are not permanent; we walk with confidence in 1991 Anno Domini, the year of our Lord, the year of grace.

Let's get rid of the smudges.

Bob Killick

PS: And get writing.

ACKNOWLEDGMENTS

My aim in writing this book is to provide the reader with a picture of a woman of gold.

There is so much to cover in eighty-three years of life within which there have been sixty-four years of marriage. Obviously and firstly, the lady of the book provided the bulk of the information to which is added stories the biographer has accumulated over the years from extensive conversations.

With the quoted aim, it became apparent it was necessary to focus on specific areas rather than to provide a fulsome overall coverage. This is no small task. It was soon recognized that the book might never reach completion without the input and advice of others. When one reaches his or her early eighties, many people—teachers, mentors, and role models—have made Judy, Judy. Most seem to have long gone. With other matters occupying my mind, the book has taken over six years to complete.

To name just a few of the people who have contributed to her life, and thus to this book, there are Judy's brother John Gillies and his wife, Fay, and Elisia Killick, who delved most successfully into the archives of country newspapers.

Another Dimension

Judy's life would have been different if it had not been for her conversion under the ministry of the layman Trevor Anthony. This was followed by great teachers like the Rev. Neville Horn and Dr. Geoff Blackburn. Another was the Rev. Bill Brown, with whom Judy and I have worked for forty-five years and have learnt that unity in the work makes all the difference.

Judy particularly wants to thank my Christian brothers and sisters at the Syndal Baptist Church with whom we have shared a journey of forty-three years and who bore with and taught me the ways of being an effective lay elder of the church.

Where Rubber Hits the Road

I wish also to express my appreciation to those who were brave enough to read the earlier versions of the book and make constructive suggestions. These include Elaine and David Oliver, Edith Ellis, and Elisia Killick.

Illustrations

For those gentle readers who live their lives through adages, it would be no surprise to hear that "A picture is worth a thousand words." When the author considered setting the tone of each chapter with a sketch, there was also the proverb, "Easier said than done."

When considering how to make it happen, there are many who have skills, for example, to be a nurse, but no one could come to my mind who was an illustrator. But talking with our registered nurse Wendy Miles, the conversation drifted to Judy's book and the setup for the start of each chapter: heading, a couple of proverbs, a sketch highlighting different aspects of the chapter's contents, and then away the author could go with his next thousand words.

Knock me over with a feather, but Wendy said, "I have over five hundred drawings which have emerged over time, helping me handle my two fights with cancer and other life challenges. They always reveal something to me, but they are just my doodling. I don't know whether I could provide sketches of each of the chapters about Judy. But nothing ventured, nothing gained." She returned after considerable collaboration with a couple of prescribed illustrations. "I think we've done it; I think we've done it!" And so we had, but for most of the chapters don't ask how much time they took to get to the standard Wendy had set herself.

Let me complete the above by saying I have learnt touches of what makes an artist, and Wendy has learnt ways to complete a prescriptive sketch without doing twenty attempts for each. Thanks, Wendy, for the stimulating time and the patience you have shown.

Please enjoy them on the way through. Some chapters are more of a challenge than others as I have also learnt.

PS: My favourite sketch is chapter 3's, and Wendy's favourite is chapters 10, 1, 7, and 8…that is an artist for you. Judy's encouraging response was, "I love them all."

While I owe my thanks to each of these people and have benefited from their input, the final missive, with its errors, belongs to me. I am ever reminded of the many years that each morning as I was leaving for work, Judy, my beloved wife, would grab me by the lapels, shake me like a wet rat (there is nothing quite like being shaken like a wet rat), and advised, "Just remember, all wisdom does not lie with Bob Killick. *Sic transit gloria mundi* (Thus passes the glory of the world)."

Judy: Chronology of a Life

Judy born September	1939	Orange Base Hospital, NSW
	1940	May, AMP promotes Mal to Newcastle
March, Judy's brother, John, born	1941	Freda strong dislike to accommodation.
	1942	March, Mal to war effort, Tenterfield, NSW. Freda, Judy, and John return to Orange as quickly as they could.
	1943	
Kindergarten	1944	
Preps (primary school)	1945	June, Mal is discharged from army.
Chatswood Primary 1	1946	May, family moves to Chatswood, Sydney.
Chatswood Primary 2	1947	
Chatswood Primary 3	1948	
Chatswood Primary 4	1949	
Chatswood Primary 5	1950	
Chatswood Primary 6	1951	
Secondary Home Science School, Manly	1952	
Secondary Home Science School, Manly	1953	
Secondary Home Science School, Manly	1954	Finishes school with Intermediate Certificate.
Begins working as speed typist at the Bank of NSW.	1955	Starts night school to obtain Leaving Certificate.
	1956	
May, enters Balmain Teacher's College.	1957	October, commits her life to Christ.
	1958	
May, graduates primary teacher, posted to Lithgow, NSW.	1959	December, returns to Manly for wedding.
January, Judy marries Bob.	1960	Posted to Balgowlah Heights School. December, Jenni born.
	1961	Types Bob's 223-page PhD thesis.
April, "Orsova" to UK for Bob's work.	1962	Rents the Wirral on New Chester Rd.
Chimney fire	1963	May, Andrew is born.
April, "Arcadia" returns to Sydney.	1964	Settle into Balgowlah, 77 Woodland St.
	1965	
	1966	
	1967	May, Peter is born.
	1968	

October, flies to UK for Bob's work.	1969	Settles into Bromley, London.
	1970	
April, returns to Melbourne via the *Arcadia* around the Cape of Good Hope.	1971	Quickly settle into Mt Waverley house and Syndal Baptist Church.
	1972	
	1973	
	1974	
	1975	
Dad, Malcom, dies in November.	1976	Gospel Theatre, youth group leader
	1977	
	1978	
	1979	
	1980	"Singing Christmas Tree"
	1981	
	1982	Judy returns to teaching when Bob is unemployed. April, Judy and five others spread the gospel from a Launceston (Tasmania) church.
March, purchases Victorian Chemical Co. on mostly borrowed money. Judy is one of the directors.	1983	Judy feels family would be tent-living if the purchase was unsuccessful.
The sales of Ee-muls-oyle, a grape-drying-oil, introduced us to products used in agriculture.	1984	November, first sales visit to Mildura to clear old stock and start yearly store managers' dinners, which lasted until 2002.
Struggle years	1985	
Struggle years	1986	Ee-muls-oyle is advertised on TV.
Struggle years	1987	Judy and Bob travel around the world promoting the grape-drying-oil.
Struggle years	1988	
	1989	
	1990	
Judy finds her niche during conferences, business meetings, and so on, being able to communicate with anyone on all management levels.	1991	
	1992	Ee-muls-oyle receives US FDA approval.
	1993	
	1994	
	1995	Judy is amazed that December sales pass $1million.

Vicchem obtains HASTEN patent.	1996	Mum, Freda, dies.
	1997	HASTEN sales building up steam with the patent under our belts.
	1998	
Judy's personality promotes Vicchem.	1999	
	2000	
	2001	
	2002	
Coolaroo negotiations.	2003	November, Dandenong factory is purchased.
	2004	December, Coolaroo factory is purchased.
	2005	
	2006	August, Richmond factory is sold following Judy's advice—make and sell chemicals.
	2007	
	2008	
Judy's seventieth birthday.	2009	
	2010	
	2011	
	2012	
Bob's seventy-fifth and Andrew's fiftieth birthdays, VCC's eightieth birthday, owned for thirty years.	2013	Bob retires.
	2014	December, Judy has a mini-stroke resulting in slight dementia.
	2015	
	2016	
	2017	
	2018	
Judy's eightieth birthday.	2019	
Judy and Bob's sixtieth wedding anniversary.	2020	
	2021	June, Judy's back vertebrae is fractured.
	2022	June, Dandenong property is sold.
October, family celebrates the forty-year anniversary of Vicchem ownership.	2023	
	2024	

INTRODUCTION

We met at nine—We met at eight,
I was on time—No you were late,
Ah yes, I remember it well!
From *Gigi* by Learner and Lowe

As this biography was being written, it became apparent how much a biography turns visceral memories into a written storage bank memory. But in the writing experience, questions arise such as what of the eighty years has been remembered, what has been forgotten, or what may be even more frustrating, what might be false memories? One becomes philosophical and realises one can only do one's best. So what, overall, are some of the aspects this eighty-year-old lady has that have provided her with the nickname of "Woman of Gold"?

The Broad Sweep of a Picture

In the broad sweep of our mind's picture of Judy, a woman of gold, we perceive a lady who has handled the mundane and challenging ups and downs, the unexpected, and inexplicable vagaries of life. A wife of sixty-four years' marriage who has survived with ease, indeed, loving it—a wife who has stood by her man for better, for worse, for richer, for poorer, in sickness, in health, to love, and to cherish. A mother who produced a trio of cheerful youngsters and remained sane during their teenage years, a comforter over their university days—and now the eldest has just turned sixty-three whilst the other two are not far behind. All are married, and each couple has two children—with the two eldest grandchildren married, and three great-grandchildren have arrived. She's been a director of a chemical company without knowing anything about chemistry yet most gainfully employed, an elder of our local church with a caring heart and loved by many, a philanthropist who recognised where help was needed before most other people, and a sportswoman of renown with the catch-cry, "Who's for tennis?"

Some of the Significant Brushstrokes

In this chapter, the following are only teasers to Judy's memories that are described more fully in the rest of the book:

- The thrill of passing the Leaving Certificate, which gave Judy access to teachers college.
- The time when I became a very serious boyfriend.
- The marriage proposal at Oxford Falls.
- The several "kitchen teas" leading to our marriage in our bedecked church; Judy was young when we married but carried five years' of work experience into it.
- The move into our first home.
- The birth of Jenni, our first child.
- Judy's typing of and seeing the completion of my 223-page PhD thesis.
- The happiness when I had my first job with Unilever.
- Our six-week trip across the Pacific and the Atlantic Oceans to get to my English research position.
- Andrew's homebirth.
- The return to Manly for Peter's birth.
- Finding and enjoying the pleasures of music as a pianist and a soprano.
- Setting up Bible studies in our English and Melbourne homes.
- The arrivals of six grandchildren.
- The emotions aroused in those Gilbert and Sullivan nights.
- The excitement of developing the Punch and Judy Travelling Show.
- The time she found herself enmeshed in our privately owned Victorian Chemical Company and not being "just a pretty face" at third-party business meetings.

Those are just some of the events that turned Judy into a woman of gold.

"It-t-t-t's Sho-o-o-ow-time!"

Moving into the biographical trail of the "lady of the house," it was a question of how many words might come to mind by asking Google, "What is a mother?" The system claims that a lady, looking for a job outside the home, might include forty-two skills she could put on her CV! As the book has progressed, this is not difficult to believe! The standard joke has always been, "Behind every successful man there is a surprised wife," but it is better written that "Behind every successful family there is a surprised husband!" Show business producers are always looking for potential thespians who have that X factor, that indefinable "something" that makes for star quality. Judy has this quality inherent in her makeup.

I sense the start of the book proper, so as we move into it, let the biographer slip into his thespian cloak and provide the call to the audience: "Sit back, read, and enjoy.

"It-t-t-t's Sho-o-o-ow-time!"

AUTHOR'S INVITATION TO THE READER

At the beginning of each chapter, please take a moment to consider the illustrated vignette by Wendy Miles (signed wfm), they are designed to give, as David quoted earlier, "merely corroborative detail intended to give artistic verisimilitude to an otherwise bald and unconvincing narrative"*(The Mikado)*, thereby providing the story with warmth, charm, and whimsy. Wendy and I trust you will find in them a hint of what's to come.

At the end of each chapter, you may wish to review the vignette once again to see how much more you now understand. Look upon them as a little bit of fun along the way.

Enjoy!

CHAPTER 1

Five Foot Two, Eyes of Blue

As the tree is bent so grows the tree.

—Anonymous

You're not turning 84 years old; you're turning 21 with 63 years' experience added.

—Encouragement on an old-age birthday card

Clear the Decks

That First Year.

For everyone reading this book, and indeed for all who live on the earth, there is the one certainty of life: We were born with the DNA that makes us who we are.

Not to be outshone, the body carrying the DNA that became Judith Helen Gillies, arrived in September 1939 at the Orange Base Hospital with the body weighing in at six pounds twelve ounces (3 kilograms or 3,062 grams). And do not be surprised, gentle reader, that her unique ragbag of genes would turn her into a woman of gold.

How Does One Bring up a Child?

A long-standing quotation in education says, "Give me a child until he is seven and I will give you the man." Perhaps it is not to be encouraged to go blindly against this claim of the ages considering the quote has been enunciated by Aristotle (384–322 BC). The quote was much later claimed by Francis Xavier (AD 1506–1552), the founder of the Jesuits. However, these long-standing teachings certainly did not stand in the way of modern scientific workers in the field as science has continued to explore. One school of thought pushed in recognition is that before the age of three, the brain forms one million neural connections every minute. It is then treated as obvious that the first three years are the most important. Then there is the school that claims it is the first five years that are most important for over this time, the child learns appropriate behaviour, boundaries, empathy, and many other social skills that will remain with them for life.

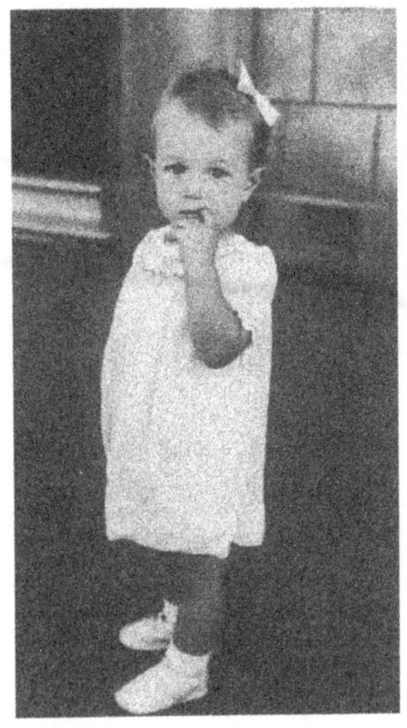
Contemplating the future.

Notwithstanding all the body is naturally doing, what it is supposed to be doing, full acknowledgment should be given to the importance of the work the parents put into training and shaping the lives of their genetic offspring. The new human is to become more than genetic clones but to become responsible mature adults who make unique contributions to the world.

Once these earliest years are complete, the unobservable traits held within their respective genes are finally fully nurtured. And by the teenage years, decisions for life are being made.

Ignoring the odd exceptions, for most people, the courses of their lives have been set by the time they are twenty-one years old. The chapter epigraph about turning eighty-four was manifestly true for Judy, only with twenty-one and fifty-nine years of experience. The years of 1939 to 1959 moulded Judy. This is only twenty years, but this time is suggested as Judy was married in January 1960, within which another moulding process takes over. Some people argue that older married couples start to look like one another if not visually but certainly by personalities.

So we can consider many of the events and experiences in the first twenty years that shook up the genes recipe that mixed and "baked" itself to make Judy, Judy—the woman of gold.

Education

Primary School

Not that Judy knew anything about it, but she was soon practicing the nomadic lifestyle. In 1940, before she was a year old, her father, Mal, had been promoted by his employer, the Australian Mutual Provident (AMP) Society, to work in Newcastle, NSW, about two hours' drive north of Sydney. This city was known as a heavy steel producer and coal by-product manufacturer. Freda loathed the location, the paucity of accommodations, and the lack of friendships. This repugnance to the living area where she found herself produced differing events. The *pièce de résistance* occurred a month or so after the promotion communiqué with Freda falling pregnant. With all this happening eighty years ago, there can only be speculation on the actual driving forces. However, it was a welcome blessing when John, a younger brother for Judy, was born in March 1941 at the Orange Base

Hospital. John has been a blessing to many people with his ministry as an anaesthetist.

Meanwhile, back at the Newcastle ranch on the third of March 1942, the family was hit for six with Mal called into the war effort to work in Tenterfield, NSW, where he was given the role of clerk. When Mal left Newcastle for Tenterfield, the family apocryphal history has it that Freda, Judy, and John were on the next train back to Orange to live out the war over the next three years.

In 1943, it was reported that Mal had received first-class results in rifle tests, and it also appeared that during the same year, he reached the rank of sergeant. Holidays were granted, and the following photo was taken in 1944 when Judy was around five years old. Judy still remembers the red frock she was wearing.

We have been very fortunate that Judy and John have enjoyed congenial family ties, doing many things together over the years. John set out to be a doctor, later becoming an anaesthetist, and married a registered nurse, Fay, in 1965. So they are one year short of sixty years married at the time of this writing. It still amazes us that a brother and a sister have enjoyed full marriages on either side of sixty years. Our visits from Melbourne have always been welcomed with shared enjoyment of their swimming pool at the rear of their property or down at the Manly surf.

Family visit, 1944.

The excitement was palpable for Mal's discharge from the Imperial Military Forces on June 9, 1945. However, he did have a bad ulcer and was sent for several months into repatriation for returned soldiers at the Country League facility in Orange. Realisation became apparent to both Freda and Mal that their time of remaining in Orange was limited. Hopes of Mal working for his father's men's clothing shop had faded with his father became blind. It was still a complete surprise when his father up and sold the business. Mal did recognise that he had a strong ability at selling insurance. Sydney was the large market, so to Sydney they must go.

The other confirming event to lead them to the big city east was that Freda's brother-in-law, Harry Beveridge, was being posted as the Commonwealth bank accountant to Bellingen, thirty-five kilometres south of Coffs Harbour, NSW. This meant their existing rental accommodation would be empty. Nothing, however, is that simple. Throughout Sydney, emergency housing was everything with blood and tears being shed to get a family's foot through the rental door. Using their in-laws, Mal's acumen came to the fore. Once the rent had been paid and the Beveridges were leaving through one door, the Gillies moved in through the other entrance without anyone knowing. They probably had not read Gilbert and Sullivan's *Pirates of Penzance*, but the spirit was extant.

With cat like tread, upon our prey we steal
In silence dread, our cautious way we feel

No sound at all, we never speak a word
A fly's foot fall, would be distinctly heard

By May 1946, the Gillies family had moved into 25 Wood Street, Chatswood. This was near the North Shore train line of Hornsby to Sydney. Mal continued his work for the AMP Society, but for Judy and John, the Chatswood Primary School was even closer than the rail station. Primary school was not completely uneventful as John was small in stature for this age and occasionally bullied. When older sister Judy was found anywhere nearby, John's guardian angel would send the bully packing, or as Rudyard Kipling phrased it, "For the female of the species, is more deadly than the male." See the Tigeress in the yearly class photo below. Her mother Freda was the only one who felt she had been given the raw prawn as she had to walk up the hill to get to the shops and come back downhill loaded. The location was soon labelled "Gillies Gully."

Judy's primary class 5A.
(Judy, bottom row, fourth from right)

There follows the copy of a letter ten-year-old Judy wrote to her grandparents following her return to Chatswood from a holiday in Orange.

25 Wood St.
Chatswood
18th May 1949

Dear Nannie and Popeye

We had a lovely trip down.

We miss you both very much and are looking forward to seeing you again soon.

Peter (Yes it was the cat) was very glad to see us and had been eating ever since.

We went to music today and Miss Benson* said we are doing very well.

I hope Popeye's cold is better and you are better too.

Lots of love
from Judy xxx

*Judy and John's music teacher was Mrs Cross, and it is now assumed she started out as Miss Benson.

An Explanatory Interlude

An explanatory paragraph is helpful before becoming enmeshed in the following secondary school section. Due to the ever-continuing citywide problems of the emergency lack of accommodations, governmental rules were modified that limited the time renters could stay in government housing. People had to be prepared to move on or at the minimum, be building their appropriate accommodations. Having had two extremely poor renting choices in Newcastle and Chatswood, the obvious answer was to find a block of land nearest to Manly Beach. Why was Manly chosen? The simplest answer was because it was the locale for the Gillieses' yearly summer holidays, and if one lives there, one can enjoy the year-round experience.

The first challenge was that Manly and its environs were being rapidly built outwards. Mal was able to purchase 20 Plant Street, Balgowlah, about four kilometres west from Manly centre, with the added benefit of a view that you could kill for. The second challenge was that it was an overgrown wilderness with lantana and blackberry bushes higher than the family was tall. The following record written by Freda has surprisingly survived the years in the archives and reflects the first day the Gillieses worked "on our Selection." This expression sprung up in the 1860s, when the governments legislated to obtain closer settlement throughout the country. It came into city consciousness with the publication in 1899 of a series of twenty-six sketches titled "On Our Selection" by Steele Rudd. They spawned a film and a series of radio programs telling of the vicissitudes of rural living in the mythical Snake Gully. The Rudd family consisted of wise Dad; dependable Mum; their son, dopey Dave; and his girlfriend, long-suffering Mabel. The theme music that opened and ended each episode was, "The Road to Gundagai."

The Gillieses had enough of rental accommodation. This was going to be their own home on their property. Here's Freda:

> Last year, 1950, we purchased a block of land—beautiful view overlooking The Spit, Middle Harbour, and Clontarf! It was covered in dense undergrowth, and

on Good Friday 1950, we started off to clear it—Mum and Dad, Judy and John Gillies.

We left 25 Wood St, Chatswood (Gillies' Gully) clad in our oldest clothes armed with various kinds of implements.

It was a lovely day, and the view from "Our Selection," Plant St, Balgowlah, was at its best—blue shimmering waters with small sailing boats dotted here and there making reflections in the water, and traffic coming down Beauty Point Hill and across the Spit Bridge looking like a line of ants in the distance.

Our next problem was where to begin the clearing operations. It was impossible to see exactly the formation of the block because of the undergrowth, but according to the agent, there was quite a drop from street level and then a fairly flat level strip to build a house on. A large rock on the side of the block was ideal, he said, for a garage.

Dad Gillies was all for starting operations from the centre of the block and hacking our way to the street; Mum had bad thoughts of spiders and snakes and preferred to begin from the street. Dad, however, won the day.

We gingerly wended our way down through the next-door block of land where there was a slight track and fought our way through blackberries and bushes into the centre of our block, where the bushes etc. were well above our heads. The thought of spiders and snakes was very frightening, and Jude and John were ordered to stay up top out of harm's way. However, after hacking away for an hour or so we soon forgot about spiders and snakes. Our objective was to make a lane-way through to the street. We uncovered several large rocks and eventually reached a retaining wall of cut stone evidently built by a former owner years ago. Mum was by this time thoroughly exhausted and covered in blackberry scratches etc., so Dad finished the cutting through to the street. By this

> time the light was beginning to fade, and our view turned to Fairyland as it became darker, and millions of small twinkling lights appeared across the water. It was just as beautiful at night as in the daylight—so ended our first day "On Our Selection."

To misquote the biblical expression of Matthew 26:41 that "The spirit is willing but the flesh is weak," the dominant quote amongst the building profession in the postwar years was, "The desire was keen, but the building materials were unavailable and the builders were few!" The family was fully involved in "the build," and seventy years later, Judy and John still remember the Saturday they moved six hundred bricks to the building area from the bottom of the chute on which the bricks were first moved twenty metres down from their delivery point. Once Mal felt he had broken his back, but fortunately, he hadn't; it just felt that way.

Early in the build, one set of builders overcharged to an incredible degree, and Mal fired them on the spot. At the critical moment to save the build, two Dutch builders turned up, and the project could be taken through to completion. They were particularly hard workers who, after World War II, had immigrated to Australia and taken on the good Anglo names of John and Charlie. It is not said that Mal spoke "Double Dutch." It just sounded that way when professional builders have different ideas than the one who is paying the money and wants the two-storey building to be upside down. This means the sleeping level is on the ground floor and the living level on the upper floor with the commanding views far left (east) centre/east over Middle Harbour to Balmoral, whilst far right (west and out of photo), over The Spit. As Freda had described it earlier, the guests felt they were in Fairyland. Perhaps one could say it was a good place for Judy to practice since her future life metamorphosed into "Alice in Wonderland."

Halfway built.
(View looks over Middle Harbour to Balmoral and far left to Middle Head.)

Secondary School

Judy's primary school world was finishing in December 1951, and secondary school awaited. It was anticipated that she would attend the Willoughby Girls High School. However, around Christmas 1951, Chatswood was farewelled, and henceforth, the family would be living at 20 Plant Street, Balgowlah. For the last days of January, Judy had three weeks within an itinerary from Balgowlah on the 144-bus to St Leonards, train to Chatswood, and bus to Willoughby Girls. It took over an hour to get there and the same to come home. To attend the Manly Secondary Home Science School was a quarter-hour bus ride. The family agreed that Home Science would be enough, so to Manly she went.

In 1952, her first year at high school, she came first out of 198 scholars in English and dictation, but at thirteen, she was painfully shy. This reached its apogee the day she was asked to come to the front of the physiology class and explain the circulation of blood through the body. It was not a question of her not knowing the answer. Rather, it was her lack of confidence that had her mouth opening and closing without any sound coming from it.

It was standard practice to have the midyear and the yearly examinations.

Manly Secondary Home Science School
Yearly Examination (1953)

PROGRESS REPORT

on Judith Gillies Class 2C2

Yearly Examination November 1953

Position in Year 10 Number of Pupils in Year 188

SUBJECTS	Percentage Gained	Position in Year	REMARKS
English	79	4/188	Very good indeed.
Dictation	100	1/188	Excellent
History	61	42/188	very satisfactory
Geography			
General Mathematics	83	6/188	Excellent work C.J.
Physiology	71	34/188	Very pleasing. has worked well. W.H.
Home Economics			
Needlework	55	99	Works well in class. L.P.
Art	54	61/187	Works well in class. Ph.
Business Principles	70	18/108	Done good work all year. W.H.
Shorthand			
Typing	90	22/188	Splendid work done. W.H.
Total	663		
Av. Percentage	73.7	7% 70.	

ATTENDANCE from 1-7-53 to 25-11-1953 3 days absent

PUNCTUALITY Excellent

CONDUCT Excellent

PHYSICAL TRAINING A reliable capable & very keen leader

SPORT Tennis Swimming

It says it all in that tennis and swimming appear in each sport.

Reverse Side
Yearly Examination (1953)

ADDITIONAL STAFF REMARKS Has worked well throughout the year. E.D.Y.

PRINCIPAL'S REMARKS A very pleasing report!

PARENT'S COMMENT AND SIGNATURE I am pleased with Judy's report, but she needs to improve with art & needlework.
F. Gillies

Teacher's Initial E.D.Y.

Date 4 12 1953

Teacher's signature E.D. Yates.

Principal C Burns

Judy thought her mother's comments quaint as Freda said "Judy needs to improve with art and needlework." Freda did not have a stitch of art in her fabric.

In 1954, her third year, Judy maintained her good standards—seventh in the school, second in Business Principles, and again first in English and dictation. Judy held the position of Vice House captain, and the shyness had drifted away. One of her roles was to address the school each morning that classes were about to begin and put one of Sousa's marches onto a record player so the pupils could march into class. For those with an insatiable curiosity, the march was either "The Liberty Bell" or the "Washington Post March," but Judy feels her memory is playing tricks as to which was the actual one.

In September, she passed typewriting with distinction from the Incorporated Phonographic Society of Australia. In December, the school also awarded her a certificate for consistently good works in typing. This skill has been well used for the rest of her life, although her firm strokes do not go well today with the modern electronic keyboards. At the end of 1954, she was granted the State Intermediate Certificate in the following seven subjects: English, history, Elementary Mathematics, Business Principles, Physiology and Hygiene, art, and Needlecraft and Garment Construction. This last subject has also been of value, allowing her to make much of her clothing.

Manly Home Science did not cater past the Intermediate Certificate, and this required Judy to attend the nearest Willoughby Girls High School. Although it may be labelled "nearest," the reality was from there to Plant Street took one hour of travel each way, every day. Added to this, Judy was not particularly enamoured with the various subjects offered. At the end of three weeks, there was a family conference that decided spending another two years to chase down the Leaving Certificate was not in her future.

The attached Intermediate Certificate became her passport to the big wide world.

NEW SOUTH WALES
DEPARTMENT OF EDUCATION

Intermediate Certificate

It is hereby certified that

JUDITH HELEN GILLIES

of MANLY HOME SCIENCE SCHOOL

has satisfactorily followed an approved Secondary Course, covering at least two years, and has reached a standard acceptable to the Board of Secondary School Studies in the following SEVEN subjects:—

ENGLISH	HISTORY
ELEMENTARY MATHEMATICS	PHYSIOLOGY AND HYGIENE
BUSINESS PRINCIPLES	ART

NEEDLECRAFT AND GARMENT CONSTRUCTION

KH

Examined and Verified.

Director of Secondary Education.

Director-General of Education.

SYDNEY: 2nd MARCH, 1955.

N.B.: This Certificate is given without alteration or erasure of any kind

Vale Academia

Choosing a Vocation

The Bank

The first question was where Judy would find gainful employment. At fifteen years of age, it was a no-brainer that with her typing prowess, it would be in a work area that required this expertise. Her father, Mal, had contacts in the Bank of New South Wales, then known as "The Wales" and today as Westpac, and Judy bypassed the typing pool to be in the Northern Rivers section as the girl Friday or, using the language of the era, the "Flossie" of the Northern Inspector's Office. Judy is the lady to have on a trivia team if there are questions on the towns and rivers of northern NSW.

A lifelong friend from those days is Jan Rowland (née Humphreys), and both of them used to take part in the corps de ballet in the bank concerts such as "Maid of the Mountains" and "Sally." The Wales ran these concerts for employee esprit-de-corps, and they were certainly up Judy's alley—straight natural casting.

The Teaching Profession

After a couple of years, Judy felt she had learned all that was needful to know about the Northern River areas of NSW and that she could be more productively utilised as a primary schoolteacher. As a cynic once remarked, "People become teachers from natural casting. They are control agents." Hello, Judy.

To get into teachers college, it was necessary for her to obtain the State Leaving Certificate with a pass in a minimum of four subjects. While she continued to work in the bank, she attended Fort Street Girls High School five nights a week. This allowed her to finish the two-year course in one year. Welcome back to academia! She recalls those lazy, crazy, hazy days of summer when the family would take off for the beach to have some fun and relaxation, and she would remain at home to study. Her perseverance showed through this period of study. Winston Churchill perhaps summed it up best using but three words in a speech given on October 29, 1941, when he visited Harrow School, his alma mater: "Never give in, never give in, never, never, never, never."

Another interesting experience was that by taking the night classes, she was recognised as a "private study candidate." These candidates had a private area to do their examinations in the Showground buildings. But all of this did achieve her purposes, and at the end of the year, she was granted the State Leaving Certificate in the following four subjects—English, Ancient History, geography, and economics. She now had the required minimum of four passes under her belt, so she was ready to be a collegian.

NEW SOUTH WALES

DEPARTMENT OF EDUCATION

It is hereby certified that

JUDITH HELEN GILLIES

A PRIVATE STUDY CANDIDATE

attained pass standard at the Leaving Certificate Examination of 1956, in the following FOUR subjects:—

ENGLISH	"B"
ANCIENT HISTORY	"B"
GEOGRAPHY	"B"
ECONOMICS	"B"

Examined and Verified

H. S. WYNDHAM,
Director-General of Education
per:

Sydney, 1st March, 1957.

53591 5.56 A. H. Pettifer, Government Printer.

State Leaving Certificate.

The government authorities around this period were concerned about the lack of teachers being trained. As a first step, it decided to double the intake of ladies in 1957 from the standard forty in January with an added group of forty in June. For this latter group, they found a few rooms in the Western Annex of the Balmain Teachers College, situated in the suburb of Rozelle, and this was Judy's *pied à terre* for the next two years. Over this time and in the same way that Judy found a lifelong friendship with Jan at the bank, two girls from her college days—Barbara Wadson and Margery Foss—have maintained contact with Judy over the years. All eighty collegians boarded, being from the country – apart from Judy and another lass – so the tutors decided to run a dance at Newington College and booked up eighty soldier cadets. Judy's "boy" for the night was a corporal from Mungindi and was known only by that name. On the back of the ball photo, Judy had scrawled, "I was 17." The three ladies were in the second group and graduated together in May 1959 and unleashed on an unsuspecting primary school world.

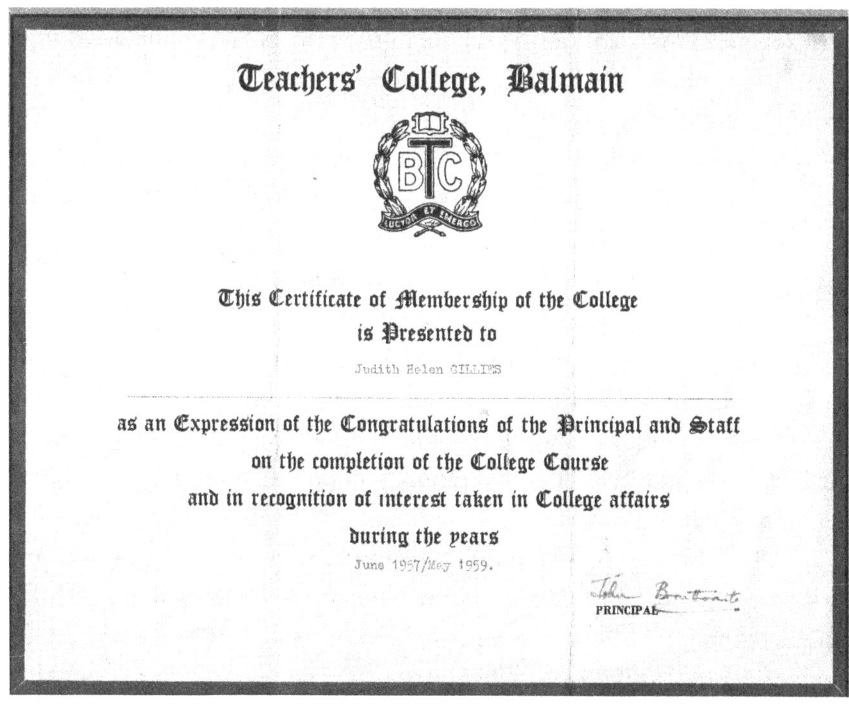

Teachers' College, Balmain

BTC

LUCTOR ET EMERGO

This Certificate of Membership of the College
is Presented to

Judith Helen GILLIES

as an Expression of the Congratulations of the Principal and Staff
on the completion of the College Course
and in recognition of interest taken in College affairs
during the years

June 1957/May 1959.

PRINCIPAL

Teachers College, Balmain.

The government's Department of Education had a series of rules to cover their provision of the free college education granted to students. The first one was that the first teaching appointment after college had to be in a country school and hers was in Lithgow, New South Wales. This city is situated on the western fringe of the Blue Mountains following the sharp descent from Mount Victoria. For interest, the city profited from the coal mines in the cliffs. The rail link down the mountainside could not be realised without the major achievement of the NSW Railways' chief engineer John Whitton, who built a zigzag rail system to negotiate the 170-metre vertical descent; it opened on October 18, 1869. This engineering feat elevated Whitton into among the top twenty greatest railway civil engineers in the first century of world railway construction.

Judy's school posting was at the Cooerwull Public School, 319 Main Street. It was also known as "Lithgow Lower" but is actually situated towards the wealthier centre. Her friend Barbara, by contrast, was posted to "Lithgow Upper." Sadly this did not mean upper class. It was a poverty-stricken area, and alcoholism was rife in the miners' lives. The derogatory comment of the area was that it was, "where the children come out of holes from the hills."

Meanwhile, back at the ranch, Margery, Judy's other best friend was posted to Cooma, which is well on its way through the Snowy Mountains towards the border with Victoria. She felt isolated during holidays, so after visiting the family home in Mittagong, she would continue north to spend time with Judy at Seaforth, on the northern side of Sydney.

At the end of the school year in Lithgow, she would return to Manly to be married. The Volkswagen was only a small car but we were still able to bring Judy, her luggage, our two mothers and a three-tier wedding cake on their laps to Manly. By chance, our honeymoon was at the Hydro Majestic Hotel at Medlow Bath, 4.4 kilometres east of Blackheath.

Barbara also appears in our annals in that the day after Judy and my marriage, we went to Barbara's family home after attending church for Sunday dinner. Whilst we were there, we scrubbed off the wedding marks such as lipstick and "Santa snow" from the car. I was very uptight that the Santa snow's writing on the duco had broken the outer-surface sheen. Not a happy Bob!

Sunday and off to church.

The other governmental rule that was planted in the students' minds was the bond that was payable if she did not remain a teacher for two years after graduation. At that time, Judy's exhilarating wage was £13 per week. Like all good governmental sets of rules, exceptions are not unknown! This was fortuitous for us as Judy fell pregnant in March 1960. Even more concerned over the bond issue was Judy's dad, Mal. It is not possible to recount the number of times he checked that the bond would not apply in the case of a pregnancy. A Scotsman ever likes to be sure.

Also fortunate for Judy was that following our marriage in January 1960, when school started in late January, Judy's posting was in a Balgowlah area school, not much more than a cooee away from home. The author's father always claimed that he knew people in the Department of Education who could arrange the right posting! Judy finished her teaching career at the start of the 1960 September school holidays to await daughter Jenni's birth in late December. On the last day, her class gave her a small thank-you present.

When the author was unemployed in 1982, there was a brief replay of her teaching prowess when Judy became an "emergency teacher" at a school near home.

Sport

Over the years, Judy has done well in all sports in which she has participated. There have been three that have been stood out during her life.

Swimming

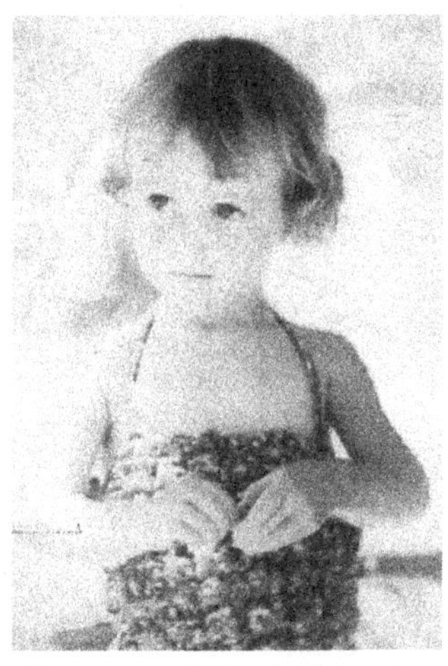

Never too early for the first swim.

Judy has always enjoyed her time in the water. She learnt to swim from two sets of teachers. The first were her parents. The second were teachers from the Chatswood Primary School who took their classes to the Roseville swimming baths.

Meanwhile, as part of the learning program at the Balmain Teachers' College, it was required to obtain a Water Safety Certificate which stated, "The Holder has satisfactorily passed the practical and theoretical tests after attending the necessary lectures and demonstrations in elementary Water Safety as laid down by The Royal Life Saving Society—Australia in the year 1957."

This was followed by the Royal Life Saving Society Bronze medallion to "J. Gillies 29.11.57." The final accolades from the Royal Life Saving Society—Australia were the awarding of an instructor's certificate dated February 5, 1958, and an examiner's certificate dated February 9, 1958. The practical end was during the 1958 January summer school holidays when Judy taught swimming to children at Mittagong, located in the NSW Southern Highlands.

Never too late for the last surf at eighty.

There was swimming in country rivers, and Judy remembers farmers' dams where she would emerge from the water with yabbies (an Australian freshwater crustacean resembling a small lobster) clinging to her clothes. This was all to the good, but Judy was still a Manly girl, and for her, body surfing was her main enjoyment and Manly surf beach the chosen one. Manly has three surf life-saving clubs at South Steyne, North Steyne, and Queenscliff. Judy and her family used to vary between the first and the last of these to set up their domicile for the day. This included beach umbrellas, cool iceboxes for drinks, hampers for sandwiches, and beach paraphernalia. It was the day at the beach!

Judy used to sunbake simply lying in the sun and would get home at night commenting, "I don't think I've tanned!" I should contrast this for myself who sat under an umbrella, slathered with sun-cream, wearing a beach shirt, towels covering my legs, grizzling after twenty minutes, "I'm turning pink. I should go home." And I never did tan. As the years past, the cost of those tanning days began to appear with the appearance of basal skin carcinomas (BSCs). These were mostly burnt off—originally with dry ice (solid carbon dioxide) and more recently with liquid nitrogen and ultimately local surgery. Judy did not have problems with BSCs until she was in her seventies. At eighty, she had local surgery for a BSC on her neck. My BSCs started in my thirties.

When together, each social group tends to talk in its own jargon. To expand on some surfing jargon, there needs to be a sidetrack on the principles of body surfing. A good wave—also known as a "roller"—occurs when the water base in an ocean swell slows down as it goes over the shallower water from the upward-sloping beach foreshores. The back trailing water continues at speed, builds up to the top of the wave, and then rolls forward. This point is called a "breaking wave." The trick is for the surfer to swim onto the top of the wave and travel with the water moving downward and then forward with the breaking wave. It is exhilarating to feel the ocean energy propelling one's body into the shore. It is this gentle upward slope of the ocean floor that determines the reputation of a beach like Manly as having good waves. However, steeper slopes can form at times due to currents, tides, and swell size, and the resultant waves can break suddenly and dramatically. They are labelled "dumpers" and it's not a good feeling to be on top of a wave one moment and on the sand the next with water pounding over you. This experience is either called "eating sand," or more often, "Going down the mine."

One traditionally mooched around in the fairly limited area in which the rollers broke, and the most stimulating call was to hear, "Out the back!" This occurred when a larger swell had been sighted, and one had to swim further out from the limited waiting area to hopefully catch the big one, which would break that much further out to sea.

Not that this book would want to leave readers feeling they would never want to go near a surf beach again, but the last piece of jargon is "the rip." This is a channel of water returning to the ocean from the spent waves. They often appear dark and relatively calm channels between the white breaking waves but result in the surf lifesavers being fully busy saving swimmers swept out of their depths in the fast, flowing waters.

We were all survivors who also say something about the following section, "Sailing, or Death in Middle Harbour."

Sailing, or Death in Middle Harbour

"We sail the ocean blue, and the saucy ship's a beauty," but as Judy and her brother, John, were only going to sail on Middle Harbour, a small sailing dinghy, such as a VJ, would have to pass muster. Judy's parents, Freda and Mal, scraped together around £35 to £39 and bought such a boat. If they had really appreciated what was swimming under the keel, the purchase might well have extended to include an outboard motor.

The VJ's history started in 1931 as the brainchild of a Mr Sil Rohu of the Vaucluse 12-foot Amateur Sailing Club. His vision was threefold: the boat was designed for two children or teenagers in which they could learn to sail and learn to race; the boat was to be unsinkable and easy to right after a capsize; and the boat could be made at home by a boy and his dad and be inexpensive.

There has been indecision on the yacht's name, but the best guess has been "Kilkie." It was twelve feet long, had a main sail and a gib, an enclosed hull, and a well in which to put their feet. Judy was the forehead hand. The sailing was exhilarating. Speeding close to the water, Judy leaned out on a board over the edge of the boat so her body weight would decrease the extent the boat leant away from the wind. This was fine until the wind suddenly dropped, and Judy was dunked into the water and hanging grimly onto the rope, being towed along behind in the water until John could turn the boat around and drag her back into the VJ. In the back of both of their minds were the shark deaths in Middle Harbour, two of which had occurred in 1942 in Bantry Bay, one off Wyargine Point in 1955, and later in the same year, another fatality in Sugarloaf Bay. This latter year was one of maximum sailing for Judy and John and thus swimming in the "shark pool" that was Middle Harbour.

A few years later, on January 28, 1963, the dangers of Sugarloaf Bay were revisited when a bull shark sank its teeth into the leg of a starlet, Marcia Hathaway, who was wading in murky water but one metre deep. After five minutes of aggression, her fiancé freed her from the shark, but she was bleeding profusely. An ambulance was waiting on the beach, but returning to the main road stalled on the steep hill. By the time the hospital was reached, Marcia had died. She had many roles in TV and radio, but her first and last movie role was in *Shadow of the Boomerang*, produced by The Billy Graham Association in 1961. She had become a Christian during the 1959 Billy Graham Crusade in Sydney.

Brother John and his wife, Fay, at full flight.

But Judy and John never saw a shark, let alone be attacked by one. John and his family went on to live at Clontarf above Middle Harbour on the rapidly rising slopes with their beautiful views back over the shimmering waters. The family purchased a thirty-five-foot cavalier yacht, *Belami*, and enjoyed many years of sailing. The boat was a size that no one had to lean over the edge, and no one ever fell in.

A bad-taste joke, but once when Judy was swimming, she saw a shark staring back at her. After a few seconds, they both turned around and went on their ways. This is known as "professional respect."

Tennis

With Judy and her mother's interest and enjoyment of tennis, consideration could be given again to the impact of genes in one's life. Why? Judy's mother's cousin was Daphne Akhurst, the Australian tennis champion in 1925, 1926, 1928, 1929, and 1930. Daphne has been honoured by the nation's tennis world by having the winner of the annual Australian Ladies Open Tennis Championship presented with The Daphne Akhurst Cup.

Daphne Akhurst.

One of the skills that contributed to Daphne's success was her ability to chase down every ball. Judy had the same tenacity, and the one joke that covered why Judy was no Daphne was that Judy had a "suspect" volley. Actually, it was a twisted knee that finally put paid to Judy's climb to Wimbledon glory, but treat this as a joke whilst noting that Daphne herself never made it to that height.

Another quote that came out of Judy's tennis years while wearing her short tennis dress, was the cry, "C'mon Legs Gillies, c'mon!"

"C'mon Legs Gillies, c'mon!"

There's No Business Like Show Business

Judy has always claimed that she was a nervous, shy girl and really felt the pressure at twelve years old when she started high school at Manly Secondary Home Science. However, by two years later, the Mower Akhurst–Ellen Tully genes had kicked in, and she became the school vice house captain. She was giving microphone announcements to the total school with aplomb. The genes had been lying dormant within the girl, and it was life in the family home under the all-pervasiveness of Freda's-always-on-the-stage environment that Judy's shyness and timidity had washed away.

Judy remembers vividly that, when she and John learnt to play the piano from ten years of age, it was naturally expected that they would entertain dinner guests or party-goers at the family home. Fortuitously, they had learnt to play the piano via the Shefte (chord) method. This allowed them to quickly be able to play the hits of the day. It soon became a regular occurrence, after the performance, to have small coins thrown to them, three pence (3d., or colloquially, a tray-bit) or even sixpence (6d., or colloquially, a zack). The coins were silver (50 per cent), copper (40 per cent), nickel (5 per cent), and zinc (5 per cent), but definitely no mention of gold.

In contrast, there is the history of the recitals provided by, to give her full name, Maria Eliza Dolores Rosanna Gilbert from Limerick, Ireland. She came to seek fame and particularly fortune in Australia, mainly at the Victoria Theatre in the Ballarat goldfields. Her show was titled *Lola Montez in Bavaria,* and her Spider Dance had to be seen to be believed. There were as many gold nuggets thrown on the stage as there was moral outrage. No, Judy never had gold nuggets, but it was fun to have the coins of silver, copper, and some streaks of nickel and zinc.

For the show business aficionado, the applause is valued more than the coins. For the more than sixty-eight years that I have known her, stage fright has never been an issue. The gene has continued through to our daughter, Jenni, and then granddaughter Tara, all of whom will be up on the stage at the drop of a hat.

Freda was good at sewing, and fancy dress costumes were readily available. Judy has also had this trait and over the years, has made many of her dresses.

Judy also mimicked her mother's recitations and can still remember parts of "The Small Boy in the Museum" and "A Pleasant Half Hour at the Beach."

By the time Judy and I were preparing for marriage, there was no question that, if able, she would prefer to be a house-owner rather than a renter under the whim of a landlord. Her parents renting in Gillies Gully at Chatswood during her childhood had left its mark. We wanted to live somewhere within the Manly/Balgowlah/Seaforth area, and after serious searching, we bought 19 Urunga Street, Balgowlah North, in the lower-valued area of the three neighbourhoods. This was a two-bedroom, brick-veneer residence that cost £4,500. We could cover the repayments on Judy's weekly salary of £14 10s and my yearly Commonwealth Scholarship of £1,040. In retrospect, taxation also now seems to have been much lower then. A third bedroom was added during our first two years at number 19.

CHAPTER 2

We've Travelled Along, Singing Our Song, Side by Side

Life is not about waiting for the storm to pass—
It's about learning to dance in the rain.
—Vivien Greene 1904–2003

Music is the language of heaven.
—Levon Helm, 1940–2012, American musician and vocalist

André Rieu, the well-known violin-playing impresario with his Strauss orchestra, circles the world bringing joy to many. This unsurprisingly makes him a little more than being "well-off." During an introduction to one of the musical items, he told of a doctor who told him, "André, if you could bring your orchestra regularly into the hospital, the number of patients would more than halve." At another concert, he cracked up the audience with, "A waltz a day keeps the doctor away."

Let me contend that throughout her life, Judy's musical skills—pianist, dancer, and singer—with stage presence have given her the background that polished her into a woman of gold.

A Pianist

In the beginnings, a ten-year-old Judy and her nine-year-old brother, John, learnt to play the piano with a Mrs. Cross in Chatswood, a suburb of Sydney. As soon as possible, the music teacher moved the students into the classics, although there are the classics and *the* classics. Judy still has her music book from seventy years ago, and the pieces marked for learning include "Naila-Waltz," L. Delibes; "Gavotte," F. J. Gossec; "Papillon," Charles Breton; "The Sleeping Beauty Waltz," from the ballet, Tchaikovsky; "The Swan Lake," scene from the ballet, Tchaikovsky; "Scarf Dance," L. Delibes; "Danse de la Poupèe," L. Delibes; and "Dance of the Flutes," from *The Nutcracker Suite*, Tchaikovsky.

Judy's and John's hearts, however, were outside playing in the bush, not practising the classics. It happens in many families that young students begin to lose interest. On the suggestion of Mrs Cross, their mother agreed that they could continue to learn piano using the Shefte method. This technique teaches pupils to play the melody line with the right hand, and each music key had set bass chords for the left hand to play. This provided a much quicker learning method, and Judy and John were soon playing the hits of the day, such as "Goodnight Sweetheart" and "You Made Me Love You." Interestingly, the Shefte method began to lose its popularity as a valuable teaching tool not long after Judy and John had become popular-music pianists.

The world of entertainment opened for Judy, and she took to it as a duck to water. Once again, the genes from great-great-grandfather William

Mower Akhurst and great-great-grandmother Ellen (Tully) carried over the years came to life in Judy. As mentioned earlier, by ages twelve and eleven, respectively, she and John were playing the piano for dinner guests or party-goers at the family home.

After three years of tuition, the music lessons were over when the Gillies family left Chatswood for Seaforth/Manly, where no music teachers could be located. However, Judy has always had a piano in our family home apart from our two sojourns in England. This has led her to keep practicing the scales and simply playing for her own enjoyment. Since our marriage sixty-four years ago, she is used to me charging in and asking her to play various scores for me, so I can assess whether the song will fit into the next concert in production. This has increased her prowess for sight-reading and her natural playing. I always say that there are two types of pianists—those who play with fourteen keys, and those who play, with bounce, the all eighty-eight keys of the piano. She might not play with all eighty-eight keys, but Judy is certainly over the seventy level, and this certainly gave bounce to her playing. Her peak achievement was at my eightieth birthday party when she played her signature item of sixty years, "The Harry Lime Theme," and knocked the audience's socks off. She had played the item at the fancy dress ball on the Wednesday of our honeymoon, which helped us win the prize for the evening.

As my eightieth birthday party approached, Judy was becoming concerned. Not only had the musical score long disappeared, but she was struggling to remember the music links. Fortunately, she discussed this problem with a music teacher who told her to sing along to the melody and her fingers would follow along. Yes, Judy did sing, and her fingers did follow along. The audience rose psychologically to its feet for a standing ovation.

Since she was thirteen years old, Judy has not undertaken any studies on or about the piano. However, to sum her up, a music critic was listening to her play the other day and said, "Just a natural, just a natural."

The Dance

From rock cave drawings of every tribe, there is evidence that dancing takes pride of place when humanity wants to express joy. It would then seem that it is rhythm that is the basis of dance as was expressed in the Broadway musical *Sweet Charity* by Dorothy Fields:

> To feel the Rhythm of Life
> To feel the powerful beat
> To feel the tingle in your fingers
> To feel the tingle in your feet

William Gilbert of the Gilbert and Sullivan operettas was asked by an interviewer, "I believe Mr. Gilbert, that you have little or no ear for music. Don't you find this interferes with your rhythmical numbers?"

Gilbert replied, "It is quite true that I have no ear for music, but I have a very sensitive ear for rhythm: it is precisely the difference between time and tune. I am very fond of music, but I don't know a discord when I hear one; on the other hand, the slightest error in time, which would probably escape a musician, would jar gratingly on my ear."

Judy has always had strong rhythm and definitely the tingle in her feet.

Ballet and Tap Dancing

Judy has always had a liking for the ballet. This style of dance originated in the Italian Renaissance in the fifteenth century and later, in France and Russia, developed into a concert dance form. It has become widespread as a highly unique art form. Around the age of twelve, she started to learn both ballet and tap dancing at a small Chatswood dance school. After joining the bank at fifteen years old (as mentioned in chapter 1), she was soon in the bank's concerts, which included ballet sequences. In the following photo, Judy is second from the left.

The can-can from the musical Sally.

It is interesting that ballet and tap dancing got taught together. A few years ago, when the Australian Ballet was organising a new avant-garde ballet, the corps de ballet was asked who could tap dance, and over 50 per cent indicated in the affirmative. Why? The key answer seems that by learning ballet and tap together, there is the development of comprehensive dancing skills. The disparity lies in the music. Ballet is graceful and classical, whilst tap is quick-paced and entertaining. The best summary for Judy is that in our home, like on the tennis court, she is known as "Leg's Gillies."

There is rhythm that moves us and can even make a person want to dance. Drums are the real champions in terms of rhythm and, therefore, so does tap dancing in which the dancer wears shoes fitted with heel and toe taps that send out audible beats when rhythmically striking the floor in time with the music.

Whilst Judy's great-great-grandfather, William Mower Akhurst, composer and lyricist married, Ellen, the actress, Judy, the star of the show, in due course married the scientist, whose only show business abilities were producing concerts, knowing what the audience wanted, and stage presence in the role of master of ceremonies.

The Waltz versus the Fox Trot

One of the most frustrating elements in life is when the multitudes keep explaining, "But it is so easy to do!" I can count 1, 2, 3, but my foot never knows what to do at the 3. In contrast, Judy is the true embodiment of everything that's excellent in the beauty of the waltz. She sparkles. This attribute was highlighted when we were on the *Mississippi Queen* cruise boat many years ago, travelling down the American Ohio River. The boat had three mature men to provide dance partners for the large number of single older ladies who were on board looking to remember their dancing days of yore. In passing, one of the escorts said, "I would like to have a waltz with you [Judy], but I can't if your husband is here for the rules only allow me to dance with lone ladies." A little later I went to the toilet, and by the time I returned, Judy and the escort were in full flight, dancing a slow-paced jazz waltz. It provided her with a real fillip for the cruise.

Another time was on a Princess cruise during the traditional last night "Bombe Alaska" parade, during which the waiters dance around the dining room holding flaming desserts aloft and twirling their napkins. It was a jazz waltz! One of the waiters who had been serving us swept Judy to her feet for an example of the art. It had the nearby tables cheering and clapping them.

Judy has been gracious to me about my lack of ability in this specific area. She has been patient over all of our sixty-four years of our marriage and feels that I have sort of reached an OK level, although I am not relaxed during the time together. "Fun" would never be a word I would use for each experience of the waltz.

In the meantime, the moment the band commences to play in 2/4 or 4/4 timing and to which a fox trot can be danced, we always gravitate to the dance floor. Judy will cut loose on any dance style and enjoy it to the fullest. It may sound pretentious, but in the course of time, it became apparent that I, the husband, could forget the rest but enjoy the fox trot and, "Happy husband is happy wife." Whilst most of the many dance styles developed over the years had set steps that had to be followed, the fundamental step of the fox trot is just walking! The author had come into his own for he could walk in time with a 4/4 rhythm. Then add the sixty-four years of training by Judy within which steps can be improvised, the dancing can be slow (110–150 beats/minute) or fast (120–250 beats/minute), and can use any step or any tempo, giving infinite adaptability. And above all, it is your dance, and you do it however you want to dance it. That is speaking our language.

The dancing duo.

Returning to the *Mississippi Queen* cruise, it was after one of our own fully improvised fox trots when one of the escorts said, "I do like the way you Australians dance as you mix the European, Japanese, and Australian styles together so well." How little did he know the long history of the lady who could take an uncertain man and let her dancing skills illumine the ballroom. However, there are times when we are dancing that I mumble to her, "You're leading, Judy, you're leading."

Singing

For Judy's piano playing, the term "natural" was used. This is also the best description of her singing. She has always had a good voice, and being in front of an audience does not faze her. Her vocal range of two octaves is from the low F, below middle C, lifting to the high F. This allows her to sing the descant part when required. Sadly, time is catching up with her and now, when the music flows to allow descant singing, Judy has reached the point where discretion is the better part of valour.

For her satisfaction, when we lived in London (1969–1971), Judy took the opportunity to have singing lessons in the City of Bromley, Kent. She still remembers the training of breathing, "yawning," and vowel sound exercises on each note. At home, she sometimes still lets fly with the vowel-sound exercises.

Gospel Theatre

There is an old quote that if you want to be a comedian, what is important is not the joke you tell, but *how* you tell it. Similarly, if you want the audience to be emotionally with you, it is not what you sing but how you sing it! Judy has this prerequisite when on the stage. It is in her gene pool, as has been discussed earlier, which has come down from both her great-grandparents, the Mower Akhursts.

She came into her own with her role in the first of our Syndal Church's renditions over the years 1976 to 1986 of three Salvation Army musicals that were written and composed by Gowans and Larsson. The Gospel Theatre, as we became to be known, had a cast and production team of fifty to seventy people at any one time. The original thought was to do the musical *Hosea*, but this required a lead tenor, and there was no available tenor in the group. After *Hosea* fell away, much discussion the decision fell on doing *Jesus Folk*.

Jesus Folk

The first musical undertaken by our church was *Jesus Folk*. This was later seen as an inspired selection. The operetta did not have one continuous storyline but the portrayal of a number of vignettes. They are linked by what each event adds to the central theme, the most basic of evangelical themes, the transformation that Christ brings to the life of His followers.

All members of the cast, without exception, were members of the chorus. From when the musical opens to when it finishes, the cast sports colourful T-shirts carrying the inscribed words, "Jesus Folk." The directions suggest that the musical should be a family affair, and this became a real blessing for our family. For over five years, we had been a nuclear family in Melbourne. The church had provided us friendship, but it was not to be compared to the camaraderie that developed over the years during which time we became The Gospel Theatre. We laughed together, prayed together, sang together, together, together, together whilst not forgetting incidental experiences such as the mice plague of Rainbow/Hopetoun in Western Victoria. We also, if far away enough away from driving home on show night, stayed at locals' homes. We were honoured for the night meal to be served with roasted wild duck that had been shot that morning. The experience of Judy spitting out the shotgun pellets as she ate has never led her back to this "specialty" of the house.

When called on to portray a particular character, the cast member slipped off the stage to dress appropriately, played the part, returned to his or her original costume, and went back to the stage.

From natural casting, Judy was chosen to play the leader of the Jesus folk. Following each portrayal with its problem, Judy's lines followed the pattern, "Well we're supposed to be Jesus folk! What are we going to do about it?" The folk natter among themselves, and Judy's response was and which was to be said commandingly, "Get the book!" The book was a very large, mocked-up Bible, so large that it supposedly took four boys to carry it onto the stage. The leader comes up with a biblical individual who provides an answer for the person's outstanding problem. For example, there was the man of the world who felt "as dead of the dodo," and in our performance, the role was played by this book's author.

The dodo.

His problem was solved through the Bible's story of Lazarus, who was dead, resurrected, and could sing of Jesus, "He came to give us life in all its fullness." Oscar Hammerstein II once said, "It is nonsense to say what a musical should or should not be—there is only one indispensable element that a musical must have and that is music." And this song was a show stopper. For this author, this means the musical guidance would be "Vivace" with a free translation, "Give it all you've got!" The lyrics were just as stimulating:

He came to give us life in all its fullness
He came to make the blind to see
He came to banish death and doubt and darkness,
He came to set His people free
He came to set his people free

(Crescendo)

Hosea

Rejoice! Rejoice! And hear the third verse of "The Pipes at Lucknow" by John Greenleaf Whittier:

> Oh, they listened, looked, and waited,
> Till their hope became despair;
> And the sobs of low bewailing
> Filled the pauses of their prayer.
> Then up spake a Scottish maiden,
> With her ear unto the ground:
> "Dinna ye hear it?—dinna ye hear it??
> The pipes oa Havelock sound!"
>
> And now "Dinna ye hear it?
> Tis the ringing tenor voice
> As crystal clear as the dawn."

The second choice of the triage of Gowans and Larsson performances we undertook also happened to be their second script. In General Gowans's autobiography, he remembered November 1967, when the then-commissioner pushed them to write another musical, even perhaps using one of the Old Testament prophets. Hosea was chosen. The book tells of the faithfulness of the prophet to his faithless wife. They also stole Shakespeare's habit of setting a play within a play, which gave us the church youth group which mirrored Bill, the youth leader, married to Betty, his wandering wife, linking with the smooth Maurice whose suitcase was packed and ready to move her on. The inner play of twenty minutes was dressed in biblical attire, and Hosea's wife, Gomer, portrayed as a slut being sold into slavery when Hosea stepped up, bought her at the auction, and took her back into the family. The explanatory song follows, but so much is missed without the melodic line:

> If human hearts are often tender,
> And human minds can pity know,
> If human love is touched with splendour,
> And human hands compassion show,

Chorus
Then how much more shall God our Father
In love forgive, in love forgive!
Then how much more shall God our Father
Our wants supply, and none deny!

If sometimes men can live for others,
And sometimes give where gits are spurned,
If sometimes treat their foes as brothers,
And love where love is not returned.

Chorus.

In the meantime, the original group was ageing. For example, the boys' voices were breaking, the amount of time needed for studies was increasing, and there was an overall running out of puff. They only found themselves a couple of times on the road.

Spirit

The third and last musical that we were able to take on the road was *Spirit,* the sequel to *Jesus Folk.* It answered the question, "What happened to the Jesus folk when the physical presence of Jesus was removed?" The musical tells the story of how the Spirit of Christ transformed the people of Christ so that they were able to suffer what had to be suffered, sacrifice what had to be sacrificed, and achieve what had to be achieved. The telling traces the descent of the power of the Spirit on the day of Pentecost via the martyrdom of St Stephen to the calling of St Paul. The music retained its high standard and commenced the show with cornets in full blast:

What does the Spirit say to the churches?
What does the Spirit say to you?
If you have ears then hear from the Spirit
Do what the Spirit tells you to!

With an unbelievable lyrical score, there was also:

To be like Jesus, to be like Jesus,
On earth I long to be like Him
All through life's journey from earth to glory
I only ask to be like Him

The winding-up of the Gospel Theatre had two performances at Syndal in October 1983. Nothing was undertaken in 1984, and in 1985, the last full presentations were all in March at Geelong, Castlemaine, and Chadstone. More than ten years of performances had taken their toll.

The song from *Hosea* that stayed with Judy and the family was:

To a God like this, we come with gladness
From a God like this, why should we hide?
To a God like this, we bring our sadness
By a God like this, our tears are dried
With a God like this, we'll face the future
For a God like this, we'll set men free
And from this day on, we'll be His people
And from this day on, our God He'll be
And from this day on, our God He'll be,
Our God, our God He'll be.

Singing Christmas Tree

The singing Christmas tree was introduced to us by an American lady, Lynda Gail Cleveland, who had friends in Melbourne and who worshipped at our church. At the First Baptist Church, Dallas, Texas, her father had engineered the original structure and over the yearly productions had completely immersed her in all the aspects of its productions.

It has been said that "Beauty is in the eye of the beholder," and it must have been one with an engineer's eye that said, "The tree is a work of art in itself." It was 7 and a half metres wide and 6 and a half metres high. When in use, holding some seventy choir members, the total weight was over seven tonnes. This caused considerable disquiet among our original church builders as a cellar area was underneath the tree's location. Finally, the appropriate approval was obtained for the build. The total number of people involved in any way in the presentation was around 250.

The Singing Christmas Tree.

It was one thing for the build but another matter for the electrical power. The tree included 17,850 light bulbs, approximately 700 metres of festoon lighting, over 400 metres of tube lighting, 1,250 metres of light cable, and 70,000 watts of general lights. There were 40 microphone channels and 2,666 metres of audio cable. The special effects of bells and explosions included over 1,375 individually soldered globes, and over 250 candle flames had been moulded.

The opening segment of the program was entertainment designed for children yet capturing the imagination of all. The puppet presentations, particularly the puppet orchestra, were a sheer delight. The choir in the tree's show of "Home for Christmas" easily held folks' attention, and there was full agreement that the nineteen carols and songs were well chosen. In summary, the "Home for Christmas" presentation was a moving experience. The songs gave glory to God, and the message of the gospel was faithfully stressed.

At the end of the fifth tree of 1986, serious exhaustion levels were appearing amongst the cast. All the participants were volunteers apart from Lynda and Sue, with the backwash of the car accident still having its impact on them. Many of the older cast were struggling to keep up with the demands of availability every Sunday afternoon. Not that we want to quote Shakespeare necessarily, but, "Parting is such sweet sorrow," and for many, tears were shed when it was realised that the decision would be made not to proceed with the sixth tree. Lynda returned to Dallas to give input for her father. Many still talk about the tree to today, and we remember "*sic Gloria transiert mundi*" ("so the Glory of the World passes away").

Church Concerts

And this is where it all came together. Aristotle, a philosopher in Ancient Greece, claimed that "the whole is greater than the sum of its parts." To misquote, it can be claimed that Judy in full flight on the stage is greater than the sum of her diverse talents!

Do you need a secular song? "Goodnight Sweetheart."

Do you need a spiritual song? "Jesus Is the Sweetest Name I Know."

Do you need an overacted melodrama with cross-dressing? This was established as early as the honeymoon fancy dress competition. Try the Woodsman's role in *Red Riding Hood*, including songs such as "Who's Afraid of the Big Bad Wolf?" and "Baby Face."

Do you need a Negro Spiritual song? "When the Saints Go Marching In." This has become Judy's signature item over many concerts. She would sing the verses written by Luther Presley in 1937 whilst she and the group of motley backup vocalists would belt out the traditional chorus. During the chorus, Judy had the audience in the palm of her hand as she marched around the stage, singing and playing the tambourine in full flight. This included lifting her legs alternately and clapping the tambourine when it was below her leg. It gave an exuberance to the item, and the audience responded with everything but a standing ovation.

Do you need the Wild Scots to take the house apart? Judy and David are always on call, and remember it is the Scots who are always at the front, leading the British armies into battle for the last three hundred years.

Roamin' in the gloamin'.

Do you want a quiet couple singing sentimental love songs when Judy—wig notwithstanding—and David can be beefing out "Roamin' in the Gloamin'?"

Do you need spontaneity? This is where the lady is in her stage forte, and a typical example went as follows. Judy was to play "The Harry Lime Theme." The MC started by telling the audience that Judy had no sheet music for over forty years and was undertaking to play with a fading memory. Whilst the audience was in a grip of anticipation, Judy decided that the piano stool height was too low. She left the piano, went behind it to find a cushion, placed it on the stool, pummelled it down, and sat on it. Still too high. Got off and pummelled it again, comfortably sat on it, and with the job accomplished, with an overall aplomb that left the audience in modified hysterics. She then looked over towards the MC with a beatific know-it-all smirk that all could read, "I'm ready and what, pray tell, are you still gabbling on about?" The playing went well. As her finishing touch, she left the piano and wound her way off the stage like a drunken sailor. None of this had been prepared beforehand, but that's spontaneity if you want it. And Judy could always surprise.

Do you need a sandwich? People debate as to who claimed the first use of the expression, "An army marches on its stomach," whether it was Napoleon Bonaparte, Frederick the Great of Prussia, or Claudius Galen, chief physician to the Roman Army. However, it is Judy who holds the practical title. After any last practice and before the curtains went up, Judy would pull out her picnic basket to provide sustenance to those in need before "the time of battle."

Do you want an inner sense of joy radiating from the stage? Without any pretentiousness, Judy provides the requisite level of joy. She wants to make people happy, and it is simply that Judy is happy in herself.

Vol. 37, No. 52, Sunday, 27 December 1992

Those Singable Songs (1)
("The Carnival Is Over")

The Seekers was one of the most popular singing groups of their day. But nothing continues forever. At their last concert, they finished their careers with a song ever linked to their repertoire, "The Carnival Is Over."

For those of a later generation, this poignant song simply tells that since the carnival has finished in its current location, it will be moving on, and the two people who have fallen in love must separate and will never meet again.

For most of us, 1992 seems to have been a carnival of flashing lights and a whirling merry-go-round, ever faster, but certainly not getting anywhere. The nation has been in turmoil, and even Queen Elizabeth described 1992 as *annum horribilis*—a horrible year. But in just a few days, the 1992 carnival will be over?

John Bunyon, in his *Pilgrim's Progress*, dreamt that the world was a carnival and called it Vanity Fair:

for the way to Celestial city lies just through this Town where this lusty Fair is kept … The Prince of Princes Himself, when here, went through this Town … and it was Beelzebub, the Chief Lord of this Fair that invited Him to buy of his vanities; yes, would have made him Lord of the Fair, would He but have done him reverence—but the Blessed One had no mind to the merchandise and therefore left the Town without laying out as much as one cent upon these vanities. The Fair therefore is an ancient thing of long-standing, and a very great Fair.

No, "to avoid the Fair we must needs go out to the world and that is not the way." No. In one sense, this year's Carnival will soon be over only to start again on 1 January. I suppose it is the best time to consider what vanities we might have purchased whether they be, "places, honours, preferments, titles, lusts, pleasures and delights of all sorts … Silver gold pearls, precious stones and what not."

Yes, we, like our Lord, do go through the carnival of Vanity Fair. No, not like our Lord, we do partake of its vanities. Yes, as the carnival stops this year, Lord help us to see where we have loved the world to our spiritual detriment (1 John 2:15-17).

Yes, let us repent that we might live such that "those who buy something, as if it were not theirs to keep; those who use the things of this world as if not engrossed in them (1 Cor. 7:30–31).

Bob Killick

PS: Anyone want some cheap, secondhand vanities?

Vol. 38, No. 1, Sunday, 3 January 1993

Those Singable Songs (2)
("Happy Days Are Here Again")

Yes, it loses something without the music, but happy New Year to you too!! So—

Happy Days are here again
The skies above are blue again
Let us sing a song of cheer again
Happy Days are here again.

Well, will they be? That is really the question.

In the worldly sense, the above song was spawned out of the Great Depression as a rallying call to get the economy moving again, *but* that didn't happen until World War II, when the demand for engines of destruction revitalised industry. At what price? Tens of millions of dead people.

Jesus indicated in Matthew 5:1–12 that there was a happiness, even a blessedness for people with the right disposition. But let me be provocative and comment on *our* chances of being happy.

Poor in Spirit: What? In a culture that pushes the highest status of self.

Mourn: Yes, some us have or will lose loved ones, but mourning for sin, maybe peccadilloes, but sin?

Hunger and Thirst after Righteousness: Probably our best chance.

Merciful: With love of gossip and the Australian tall poppy pull-down, we may have to let this one go.

Pure in the Heart: I don't think we're going too well.

Peacemakers: At home. at work, but also to help people make peace with God.

Persecuted for Righteousness: But difficult when most of the world seems bored with us.

Well, if that's the right way to be happy, it looks like it could be one of those years.

Bob Killick

••

Vol. 38, No. 2, Sunday, 10 January 1993

Those Singable Songs (3)
("If You Knew Suzie")

Yes, many of you may find it hard to believe, but people did sing:

"If you knew Suzie, like I know Suzie
Oh! Oh! What a girl,
There's none so classy as my fair lassie …

But how well do we know anybody?

Now obviously, how little we know doesn't seem to interfere with making comments about other people. Wasn't it Max Walker who said, "Never ruin a good story with the facts"?

It concerns me that the Scriptures equate in 1 Peter 4:15 murder, thievery, and evil-doing with being a "busy-body in other people's concerns." In 1 Timothy 5:13, Paul ties in busy bodies with "tattlers/gossips speaking things which they shouldn't."

From the above, it is no wonder that James 3:1–18 highlights the tongue "as a fire, a world of wickedness … it defiles the whole body … it is set on fire by hell."

But do we really know Suzie?

But then the Bible (Phil 3:10), also talks about the knowledge of Him as our most simple and yet ultimate goal: "That I may know Him and the power of His resurrection, and the fellowship of His suffering being made conformable unto His death."

To know is incredibly important for, as Jesus said, in John 17:3, "Now this is eternal life: that they *know* you, the only true God, and Jesus Christ, whom you have sent." (emphasis added).

Bob Killick

PS: Sorry Suzie, you are probably a wonderful girl, but there is someone else who is more important to know.

••

Vol. 38, No. 3, Sunday, 17 January 1993

Those Singable Songs (4)
("Carolina in the Morning")

At a group of mature members of our congregation, I started singing some of those singable songs and they joined me; yes, over-50s stay with me for indeed:

Nothing could be finer than to be in Carolina in the morning ...

If I had Aladdin's lamp for only a day I'd make a wish and here's what I'd say

Nothing could be finer than to be in Carolina in the morning.

Well, we don't have Aladdin's lamp, and we are away from the imminent euphoria (or madness) of the New Year, so what are the wishes we might have for 1993?

After a passing reference a couple of weeks ago, there was the challenge from 1 Corinthians 7:30–31 that "those who buy something, as if it were not theirs to keep; those who use the things of this world as if not engrossed in them." So let us ignore material wishes "for the form of this world is passing away" (7:31). Yes, we live in the world, but it is not the end.

We are pilgrims for the people of faith (Heb. 11:13–16) are not yet in possession of the things promised, "but had seen them far ahead and hailed them, and confessed themselves no more than strangers or passing travellers on earth ... we find them longing for a better country."

No, I have not been in Carolina in the morning, but I confess that I believe there is something finer.

Let us wish that we might all be able to confess that we are longing for a better country ... the heavenly one. That is why God is not ashamed to be called their God for He has a city ready for them.

Bob Killick

PS: Then to see the river of the Water of Life, sparkling like crystal and flowing from the throne of God.

••

Vol. 38, No. 4, Sunday, 24 January 1993

Those Singable Songs (5)
("Heigh-ho! It's back to work we go!")

Yes, you trivial musical purists, we all know that is a verse from a song in Walt Disney's *Snow White and the Seven Dwarfs.* I can still see the dwarfs marching to the mine, silhouetted against the rising sun. My best recollection is that their approach to work was positive.

I don't know whether it is the media or an attitude picked up from people, "Thank God it's Friday," but work does not seem to get very good press these days.

Forty years ago in Christian books, we were encouraged to emulate the artisan who would spend all his life finishing some stonework high up on a cathedral where no human could see, but of course, God could. How gauche to the modern mind. We have grown up, and now our work has to be significant and where all can admire our handiwork or at least admire our status in the company.

The Bible's approach is more than provocative to the modern mindset (Eph. 6:6–8). Speaking to slaves (and I've heard enough people say they're slaves to "the system"), "obey your bosses (free translation of earthly masters) with respect and fear and with sincerity of heart *just as you would obey Christ*" (emphasis added). Now, who is having who on? My boss as Christ? "Obey them no only to win their favour when their eye is on you." Shades of *How to Succeed in Business without Really Trying*, but like slaves of Christ, not "the system," "doing the will of God from the heart." You mean the will of God is to work? "Serve wholeheartedly *as if you were serving the Lord, not men,* because you know that the Lord will reward everyone for whatever good he does, whether he is slave or free" (emphasis added).

Oh well, back to the old drawing board. Some of our previous patterns of life don't seem to be right.

Bob Killick

PS: "Heigh-ho Silver!" Woops, we're not in the Lone Ranger movie. But if silver is all you want, then silver is all you will get.

••

Vol. 38, No. 5, Sunday, 31 January 1993

Those Singable Songs (6)
("Tip-Toe through the Tulips")

To finish this series, the least we could do was to complete the round with a song that has been sung at a few church concerts.

Knee deep, in flowers we'll stay, we'll keep the shadows away …

Come tip toe through the tulips with me.

So what can one say? Tulips don't even rate a mention in the Bible, but the danger of the atmosphere does where knee-deep in flowers and no shadows follow our way. We long for ease, but the Bible stresses no!

If to be blessed is something to be desired, then woe is to be avoided at all costs. Yet Amos 6:1 could say, "Woe to those that sit at ease in the church" (free translation), whilst verses 3–6 expand on "sitting at ease." Is sitting at ease something so evil that it can be equated to "*Woe* to him who builds a city with bloodshed and establishes a town by crime" (Hab. 2:12; emphasis added)?

The scriptures use another word that parallels sitting at ease and that it is to be "asleep." The prophet Isaiah in 56:10 fulminates against those who should be its "watchmen … blind … ignorant … dumb dogs, they cannot bark; sleeping, lying down, loving to slumber."

In Mark 13:35–36, Jesus tells us to "watch! … do not let the Master find you sleeping," but here I find the theology disturbing for Paul (Rom. 11:8) reminds us that it is written, "God gave them a spirit of stupor." So it is even for Christians that Paul has to challenge us (Eph. 5:14–150), "Wake up, O sleeper rise from the dead and Christ will shine on you, be very careful, then, how you live."

Is there woe in our lives because we are tiptoeing through the tulips … even asleep?

Are we simply not being careful how we live?

Bob Killick

PS: Forget the tulips and look for the rose of Sharon and the lily of the valley (Song of Solomon 2:1).

CHAPTER 3

Wives Were Made to Love and Kiss

Marriage is an adventure, like going to war.'
—Gilbert K Chesterton (1874–1936)

A mother encouraging her daughter after her own difficulties:

> It was very difficult my dear; but I said to myself—"That man will be a mad eccentric scientist one day and I will love him. Several of my relatives said I couldn't, but I did—desperately!" (W. S. Gilbert, "The Gondoliers")

Sir Bernard Montgomery was one of the most decorated and renowned British generals of the Second World War. In preparation for the D-Day landings (June 6, 1944), he led the retraining of the British Army with utmost rigour after its demoralising retreat at Dunkirk. His classic challenge to the young soldiers under his command was, "Before you consider marriage you must be fully trained in every element of warfare."

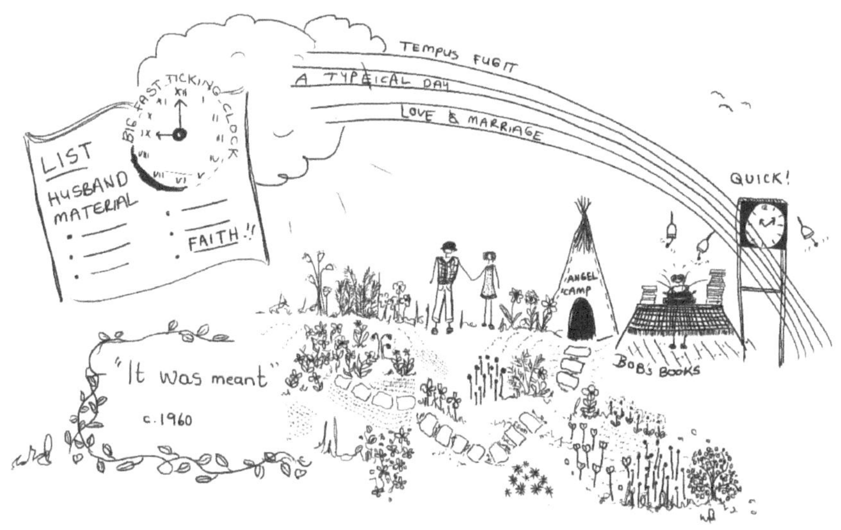

It ever became more apparent that as Judy's life continued apace, all the events that touched her life were falling into place for the furtherance of the gospel. "It was meant" had become a most quoted expression. This theme is picked up in the following Editorial. There is one major mistake in that I "forget" to include our marriage. This should have been included at the top of the list for it was an event that had to be meant!

Vol. 38, No. 20, Sunday, 16 May 1993

Non-Biblical Christian Quotes (1)
("It Was Meant")

Well, it all depends on the tone of the voice, but the way most times I have heard this expression, I cringe. However, let me stress that I can think of two major events in our family's lives which "were meant."

The first was when I had not only missed out on a major company promotion but to stay within the company, we were "sent" to Victoria twenty years ago. Just contemplate, no Victoria, no Syndal Baptist. The second was twelve years ago when I was sacked and had to find something to do. We often contemplate that no sacking, no Victorian Chemicals.

For us personally, both instances at the time were perceived as non-good, but looking back over the years, we see the incidents were more than for the best. Now all of us are trained (Rom. 8:28) to acknowledge that all things do work together for good for Christians. That is, for those who love Him, who have been called according to His purpose.

The questions do arise as to how long we have to wait to perceive something as good, and the above personal incidents might be seen as trivial when evil touches a life. The earliest classical Bible story tells of Joseph's brothers selling him as a slave into Egypt. As Joseph recounts later to his brothers, "you practiced evil against me, but God meant it for good" (Gen. 50:20).

Yes, we do want to understand what is "meant" in our lives. After the birth of Jesus and the visit of the shepherds, Mary pondered about what was happening (Luke 2:19) and don't we?

In Luke 18:35–43, we read of the blind beggar who heard the multitude and wanted to know what it meant. It meant that Jesus of Nazareth was passing by for the last time but with power to make the blind to see. It meant that through the noise, the blind beggar made his opportunity to call out.

Bob Killick

PS: In the noise of life, Jesus still passes by, and there remains our opportunity to call out.

....

The Build-Up

Judy was not a person who had an overweening belief that to be married would realise a lifelong ambition. For Judy, who was still in her late teenage years, the "lifelong" period sounded quaint. She was just simply pleased to have a night out with "a good sort" (to quote her mother). Never was there a list on which she could tick off the attributes that she considered essential for a future husband, and with whom she would have a happy married life. Having recently dedicated her life to following Jesus as her Lord, there would be one exception on the nonexistent list. Namely, whatever the future might hold, her husband-for-life would, of necessity, have to be a Christian!

The following photo of David, certainly a good sort, but most sadly, he died in his early twenties.

Judy and David.

To maintain the reader's interest in a book, this is the obvious point where an author would introduce that first meeting of Judy and the author with a flamboyant flurry. Each of us catching a glimpse across a crowded church, eyes locking, lightning flashing, and thunder rolling! But perhaps that is a little over the top.

But returning to the real world and time, we did not gaze cowlike into each other's eyes since when we first met, Judy was flat-out studying to get to teacher's college, and I was holding Margaret's hand. Judy and her mother were in agreement that "Bob Killick will marry Margaret." However, Margaret was committed to work on the mission field and left to go to the Ballarat Base Hospital School of Nursing for a three-year course rather than undertake the four years in Sydney. Rather than discussing which quote, "Absence makes the heart grow fonder," or, "Out of sight is out of mind" might be the most apposite, it must simply be recognised that Margaret's decision was meant, and both of us went on to find our marital destinies. Our relationship sputtered out after a few months, and Margaret, in due course, found Lawrie and missioned in Chad, located in the centre of Africa. David was happy to go out with Judy to the odd ball, but there was no flashing of eyes, and so on.

Once it was apparent that any long-distance romance was over between Bob and Margaret, it was that moment when Judy and my eyes were naturally ready to lock across that crowded church with full lightning flashes and thunder rolls.

I often joke with Judy by asking why she ever ended up married to me when she had 999 others clamouring around her feet to push their chances. Her only reply has been, "Forget the 999. You were the one who asked me out!" Looking back sixty-six years, Judy and I agree that the first date was to go to the movies in the Holme and the Sutherland Room in the Sydney University's Union building. Movies are still being shown there. We are in reasonable accord that it was a Swedish film, but after that, ragged memories throw up the thought between Ingmar Bergman and a travel documentary about the beauties of the country, which were quite wide-ranging and included the tallish grasses that grow on sand dunes with strategically placed sunbathers. Either way, we enjoyed our first night out. We are both good conversationalists, and it all reminded Judy of one boyfriend, Graham, who had no conversation! During the day at work, before going out at night, Judy would ask the other office girls for a list of questions she could use to stimulate "talkies." Graham, nor other protagonists, never rose to the bait, and thus neither did a romance.

Neither of us is prescient, so in our teens, we could not imagine that our future pairing might develop into The Punch and Judy Show.

The first inkling could have been noted at one of the items in a concert, produced by myself at the Seaforth Church, in which Judy, with a gun, chased a David, one of the lads from the youth group, through the audience, out the window, and back again singing, "You Can't Get a Man with a Gun." With apologies to Irving Berlin, she did get her man—not him, but me!

Life settled into the quiet rhythms of courting and, of course, there was the first big dinner date! I promised to take her to the up-market Italian Florentino Restaurant in the CBD. There were only two deal-breaking problems. The first was that I had never been to an up-market restaurant and thus did not know how the system worked. The second was that I didn't know what Italian cuisine tasted like. So I quietly worked on plan B. The night came, and my dad slipped me £20, which was more than adequate to take two people to a "flash" restaurant. Judy was ready in a red-satin frock looking like a million dollars. Five minutes from her house, I did not turn left for the city but right for what I explained was a surprise destination. It was certainly a surprise when I bought some fish and chips, which we ate on the sea cliff at the end of the Long Reef Golf Course. She was practical and used one of my handkerchiefs as a serviette to stop any fat from getting on her frock. Thankfully, none did. Judy was also noteworthy that there was not one complaint. The finale for the night was Dad had over £19/10/returned.

An aberration from the traditional courting mores was that each Saturday night we joined with the Open Air meeting in the Corso in Manly to catch the evening cinema crowd. Judy's area of activity was to hover around the back of the twenty to thirty who gathered and give outsiders a biblical tract as they tried to decamp unseen into the night, not realising they were trying to outfox the eagle eye of Judy. She also provided help when songs were sung and would give her testimony.

Will You Marry Me?

After around six months of courting, the once-in-a-lifetime moment arrived. It is time to misquote Gilbert (from the operetta *H.M.S. Pinafore*). Whilst the operetta's action had the *Pinafore* "riding anchor on the Portsmouth tide," we were out under the stars at Oxford Falls, about ten kilometres north of our Seaforth homes. The conversation, whilst not perfectly remembered, started when I gave a transcendent sigh.

> JUDY (*with concern*): Oh Bob, what a melancholic sigh! You're surely not poorly and sickening are you?
>
> BOB (*with passion*): I am poor in the essence of happiness, dearest Judy, rich only in never-ending unrest. In me, there meets a combination of antithetical elements that are at eternal war with one another. Driven hither by objective influences, thither by subjective emotions, wafted one moment into blazing day by mocking hope, plunged the next into the Cimmerian darkness of tangible despair, I am but a living ganglion of irreconcilable antagonisms. I hope I make myself clear.
>
> JUDY (*with a rapidly beating heart*): Perfectly. Your simple eloquence goes to my heart.
>
> BOB (*warming to the conversation*): Aye, even though Jove's armoury were launched at the head of the audacious mortal whose lips, unhallowed by relationship, dared to breathe that precious word, yet would I breathe it once, and then perchance be silent evermore. Judy, in one brief breath I will concentrate the hopes, the doubts, the anxious fears of six weary months. Judy, I am to be a mad eccentric scientist, and I love you desperately. My life is in your hand. I lay it at your feet!
>
> JUDY (*with joy*): Yes, yes, I love you.

And with agreement to marry being sealed, of course, with a kiss, we slipped into song: "With joy and rapture unforeseen for now the sky is all serene." Then naturally, the kissing started again.

The conversation moved to matters of state. The marriage service was agreed for nine months' time, on January 2, 1960, which allowed us to have two weeks for our honeymoon and then time for Judy to settle into our home before the summer school holiday break was over.

Preparations for a wedding can almost provide a forewarning of how successful married life might or might not be in the days ahead. A simple survey of recently married brides gave differing tensions and stresses that reach a crescendo as the wedding date approaches. Not in order of importance, they included: the choice of the bride's dress; who was to be in the bridal party; the style and colour of the clothing; how much "Aunt Matilda" would be offended if she was not asked to make the bridal cake; who was to be asked to the reception; music choice; speech-givers; venue availability and their ability to work with the bride; and most important, that the immediate families can work amicably together.

For our wedding, circumstances meant the decision-making processes were quite amicable. Both fathers were not interested in being involved in the arrangements. My mother was never in the best of health and was never going to get into robust discussions. The bride herself was involved in most of the early major decisions, but during the three months she was away up-bush at Lithgow teaching, the day-to-day decision-making fell to Judy's mother, Freda, and me. One could not get a more indomitable, effective combination. There was only one difference of opinion, which was Freda's keen desire that her daughter would have the bridal waltz and my resolute determination that I would not be dancing in it. I mean at twenty years of age, and although I was kept being told, "It is as simple as 1-2-3," my feet just didn't count that high. Judy was very gracious about it all, and whilst she is the epitome of waltzing elegance, she agreed to let the waltz disappear, and the reception would be graced by a rousing concert. During our courtship, Judy and I enjoyed watching *The Good Old Days* vaudeville program on TV. The compere himself was one of the stars of the show, and he could excite the waiting crowd with the use of actual words that were completely incomprehensible to them. His style was used to describe the upcoming reception entertainment and contain sentences such as:

> To titillate the audience it was a gallimaufry presentation having a salmagundi of styles, although terpsichorean items were held back.

The traditional speeches were still undertaken well with no one going overtime. Anyway, the key was the concert, and it was enthusiastically received. It has remained unique from all other wedding receptions we have attended over the years, particularly with no bridal waltz.

If it was true that it was Helen of Troy who launched a thousand ships, then the following invitation for Judith Helen certainly launched The Punch and Judy Travelling Show.

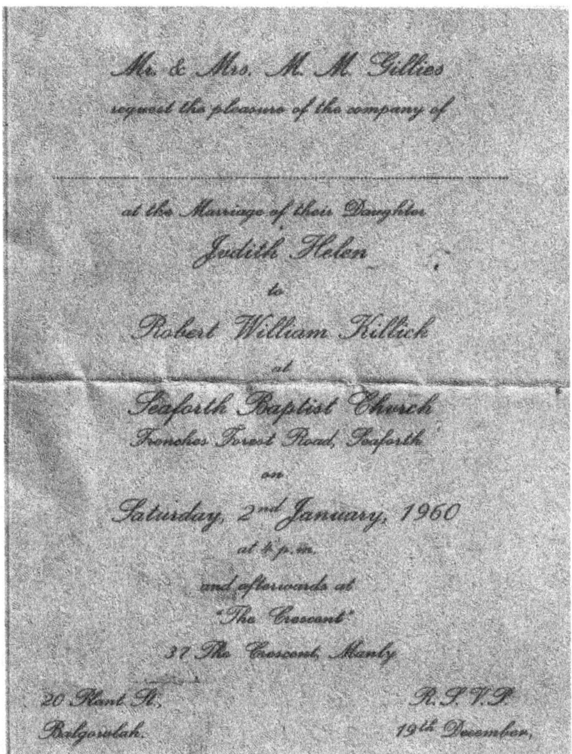

Mr. & Mrs. M. M. Gillies
request the pleasure of the company of

....

at the Marriage of their Daughter
Judith Helen
to
Robert William Killick
at
Seaforth Baptist Church
Frenchs Forest Road, Seaforth
on
Saturday, 2nd January, 1960
at 4 p.m.
and afterwards at
"The Crescent"
37 The Crescent, Manly

20 Plant St.
Balgowlah.

R.S.V.P.
19th December.

The Wedding

For the day, the recorded maximum temperature at Sydney's Observatory Hill was 31.3°C. But how hot is hot? Both Judy and I, looking at our pastor presiding over the service, saw profuse perspiration dripping from his face. Judy said later that she wanted to take one of her handkerchiefs and wipe his face. We actually felt that the temperature was running towards 40°C. Put it down to a microclimate at Seaforth.

The morning started blue skies and sunny. Judy's major project was to have her hair done, which went according to plan. As she was driving home, she saw my distinctive VW coming from the other direction. She pulled into the gutter and ducked below the dashboard. The things one does to maintain a tradition that claims the bride and groom should not see each other before the wedding service. I think we did catch a peep of each other, so whilst whatever dour disasters should have occurred if the tradition was broken were never spelt out, they never caught up with us. So much for traditions.

After lunch, Judy and the bridesmaids came to change at our Kanangra Crescent home, whilst the men went to Judy's house. This was done as Judy would not have been able climb up the garden path from her house's front door to the level of Plant Street, where the bridal cars would have been waiting. The problem lay with her tulle skirt, which was held out by a hoop 1.5 metres across at ground level. The very highly polished black wedding cars were on time. Two of the wedding photos, being mainly of the bride, showed only half of the grille of the car, and the other shot showed that window had two panes and not the soon-to-be single wrapround glass. However, from what little information was available, two car "tragics" were independently able to confirm that the bride's car was a 1948 Chrysler Windsor, but the first thing Judy saw was that there was no bride-doll on the engine hood at the front of the car. Not a complete disaster but something she has remembered even to today!

Our Seaforth church had been decked out to a T by Freda, who had been to the markets at 4 a.m. to obtain all the fresh flowers at the lowest price. Freda had made three large silver bells to hang above the aisle. These were sixty centimetres across at the base. But more important, as the service started, what did Judy and I see? Two simple quotes say it all: "She came down the aisle, wearing smile, a vision of loveliness," whilst as Judy looked ahead, "The bride eyed not her garment but her dear bridegroom's face."

The Reception

There is no debate that Judy had the reception she wanted at The Crescent in Manly with the right locale and its traditional style. It was in home territory, being strategically located not ten minutes from the church and was the right size for the 110 family and friends who gathered for the celebrations. Wedding traditions were still strong in 1960, and there had been a debate as to whether it was appropriate for Judy and I to create our own "script" for the marriage service. We did, although there were no major changes.

It became very apparent that the reception followed the traditional path when the demographic of the attendees showed 80 per cent were our parents' ages and above. This contrasts to these days, when 80 per cent would be the ages of the bride and groom's friends. The standard format was followed, with our church secretary proposing the toast for the bride and groom; the latter then cheerfully and dutifully replied with thanks and proposed the toast to the bridesmaids. This was followed by the best man giving thanks for the nice words spoken about the bridesmaids. His official finishing was the reading of the telegrams and other communications. To provide fullness, the fathers each added their two pennies' worth.

But don't forget the bridal waltz! Not to worry; it will not be forgotten. It never happened! It remains a story in the family archives that is pulled out and retold every six months or so.

But why, gentle reader, are you so bemused that the bridal waltz, such an integral traditional part of the wedding festivities, could not happen? To this type of important question, the answers are often the simplest. For example, in this case, the groom could not particularly dance but certainly could not waltz. Added to which, he had no desire to shuffle around the floor while the bride, who cuts a fine figure on the dance floor, would waltz the night away, time permitting.

But again, as you ponder, were there no ramifications in the breaking of the tradition? For Judy, the one who was most affected, not one word was uttered. Freda, Judy's mum, was the only one who volubly expressed her opinion that her daughter was going to have the bridal waltz. Negotiations were not extensive as the compromise was reached that the waltz was moved aside to make room for a concert using various members of the gathering. This included a duet from the bride and her father-in-law, "Jesus Is the Sweetest Name I Know," and, "No One Ever Cared for Me Like Jesus." The best man and one of the groomsmen provided two piano duets, and so on. The consensus for the day was that a good day was had by all, and there went the traditional world.

And the sequel happened sixty years later, on October 26, 2019, with a concert combining Judy's eightieth birthday and our sixtieth wedding anniversary. Within the items covering the latter anniversary, we had our top tenor, David Olivetti (sadly, Luciano Pavarotti had died), to sing one of Richard Tauber's greatest successes, "Wives Were Made to Love and Kiss," with some of the lyrics modified to suit the occasion. More important once a bride and groom provided the onlookers with a Bridal Fox Trot. The spelling might look wrong, but the spirit was there as a wedding dance had actually taken place!

Immediate Post-Wedding

The apocryphal folklore of the family, with sadly only a miniscule of truth behind it, starts with our departure from the reception.

The departure.

Judy had asked that, as it would crown her wedding day, if we could leave the reception by horse and buggy using Mustang, her favourite horse from her country days. I agreed, being not only wise in political correctness but learning fast in marriage correctness! So we departed, but not 100 metres down the road, Mustang tripped and fell. Without a word, Judy procured a shotgun from under the back seat, stood in front of her horse, and in sibilant, steady tones said, "That's once." She got back into the buggy, and we proceeded with me looking nonchalant in the extreme. Sadly and terribly inauspiciously, Mustang fell again although we had travelled but 525 metres. Judy responded as before, but this time she waved the gun and her voice was strident: "That's twice!" The trip did make another 350 metres when Mustang, I must believe that great horse just did not see the pothole, fell. Judy retrieved the gun, stood in front of her horse, and without a word, pulled the trigger. Mustang was no more.

She returned to sit beside me, and you will understand, dear gentle reader, that I could no longer control my tongue. I asked with trepidation, "What did you do that for?"

She looked calm and serene. And with a quiet, controlling voice said, "That's once." I immediately learnt the value of controlling my tongue, and we have had a most happy marriage as shown in the earlier comic strip.

Our friends have often said, "We can't wait for the book as we can't wait to hear of the many things that must have happened with you two." Well, we stayed at the Hydro Majestic Hotel at Meadlow Bath. The author remembers well the competitive fancy dress balls that were held each Wednesday night where you could perform an item in the costume you were wearing as per the following photo.

Honeymoon fancy dress ball.

Our song was "Tip Toe through the Tulips." and yes, we did win the prize on the first night in which the author sings falsetto, off-note, off-key, or just let's say, off everything musical. Some people would believe that it was done deliberately. The second night, the MC came up and apologised after we didn't win the prize as the house rules dictated that everyone must have a chance of winning.

Judy, having been born and living her early years in Orange, felt that it would be pleasant to spend a day visiting the city and old relatives and friends, many of whom had come down to the wedding. It was only a two-hour, 150-kilometre journey. It was planned for early in the second week of our honeymoon, but at that time, I had a bout of tinea (athlete's foot or ringworm), which made it difficult for me to drive. Not to worry as Judy could take over the wheel. I think it was interesting having Judy drive me for the first time. It was a pleasant day.

She was always a beauty.

Judy has a passion for gardening, and it wasn't soon after the return from the honeymoon that she was out mixing it in the garden. The one shown is a monstera deliciosa, the fruit salad plant.

One of the things we have learnt during our sixty-four years of marriage is the danger of small problems. As it is stated in the Song of Solomon, "it is the little foxes that eat the grapes." The following Editorials touch on small matters but remain of importance.

Vol. 38, No. 21, Sunday, 23 May 1993

Non-Biblical Christian Quotes (2)
("God doesn't sleep, He only pretends")

In all our lives, as we mentioned last week, there are times when God does not seem to be actively participating in our lives. Our most gracious judgement is that perhaps He is. Well, we often make judgements that border on blasphemy.

Now this is not new. Habakkuk cried out in frustration (1:2), "O Lord how long must I call for help before you listen?" If Habakkuk was important, how much more are we?

If you haven't noticed, one of the "in" books in our church at the moment is *Reinventing Australia*, which tells of the many changes that have occurred during our lifetimes to the culture that we find ourselves in today. The one area that does not weigh heavily in the book but impinges on the above is the craze for *instancy*, whether from instant coffee to instant health cures.

So why shouldn't God also answer instantly?

Habakkuk continued his complaint (1:12–17), reaching the point where he said (free translation), "OK I'm just going to climb my watch tower and wait for an answer (2:1). God did reply but again the message was not yet: "what I show you (Habakkuk) will come true. It may seem slow in coming but wait for it. It will certainly take place and it will not be delayed" (2:3).

Habakkuk finally prayed and toward the end could say, "I will quietly wait for the time to come when God will punish those who attack us … even though the economy is also lousy [free translation] … I will still be joyful and glad because the Lord is my Saviour (3:16–18).

It is the false gods who are asleep (1 Kings 18:27). Indeed, they have never been alive!

Bob Killick

PS: Perhaps we should ask not whether God is asleep but whether we are spiritually asleep.

Vol. 38, No. 22, Sunday, 30 May, 1993

Non-Biblical Christian Quotes (3)
("God doesn't pay His debts with money")

This quote begs the question, 'Does God owe us anything anyway?"

Not wanting to lose ourselves immediately into theology, one of the doctrines of God is His sufficiency. That is, His glory is not affected by His creation, or further, He owes us nothing!

But having created us, He does in grace provide for us such as including His maintenance of the world (Matt. 5:45) to matters that are seemingly insignificant (Matt. 10:30). So God has covenanted to owe and provide our needs for life itself (Phil. 4:19).

But deep down, most of us want to know about good, old-fashioned money. There are always enough other Christians who have testimony that they followed certain specific patterns of behaviour, and lo and behold, God was in debt to them and found it appropriate to pay them in the "coin of the realm."

Now, I struggle with this for in the most well-known excerpts (Matt. 22:15–22) of Jesus's repartee with the Pharisees, He asked for a coin and simply enquired, "Whose face and name are these?" to which there was only one answer, "Caesars." (For us, it is Queen Elizabeth). For our debts, Jesus then instructed us (verse 21) to use the appropriate coinage, dollars for our life in the world, and for God, what belongs to Him. (To consider what coinage belongs to God will have to wait for another time.)

So is there any way that God may pay us in the coin of the realm? For some, this might not seem an exciting answer, but the Bible says through work. In 2 Thessalonians 3:10, the negative is expressed: "that if any would not work neither should they eat!" Work is enjoined as the legitimate means to obtaining our livelihoods. Indeed, we are commanded and exhorted in 2 Thessalonians 3:12 to work with quietness and eat our own bread.

It is I owe, I owe, so off to work I go.

Bob Killick

PS: Simply, work remains our highest Christian privilege and duty.

....

Vol. 38, No. 23, Sunday, 6 June 1993

Non-Biblical Christian Quotes
"I'll pray for you"

I don't think there is anyone who has not had this said to them or who has not said it to someone else. In one sense, this is a great expression of love that we can show to another person. But the greatest danger is when it is only glib, loose God-talk.

The words sound spiritual, but what does it mean if it rides in an empty heart? We know that we are not to take the name of the Lord our God in vain (Ex. 20:7), and none of us would swear, swearing being too obvious. But, "I'll pray for you," can be just as profane, empty, simply empty!

What concerns me is that this does not seem to worry us. So what? I've said the right thing! What does it matter? Only God knows I didn't really follow out my promise, and He's understanding and forgiving. Isn't He?

So what happened to the old-fashioned fear of the Lord?

"So the Church," as read in Acts 9:31, "enjoyed peace being built up; and going on in *the fear of the Lord* and in the comfort of the Holy Spirit, it continued to increase" (emphasis added). Yes, I am well instructed in the Holy Spirit, but the fear of the Lord?

Somehow, the word *fear* does not sit well with love and forgiveness and grace. Perhaps it is instructional to note that the "comfort" of the Holy Spirit follows the fear of the Lord!

What is even more challenging to me is how does the fear of the Lord enter my life? Ananias and Sapphira (Acts 5:1–11) weren't killed by the Lord only a couple weeks ago. For the church then it was "great fear." Our familiarity with the holy over the years has certainly seemed to have bred contempt. How profane are we?

Bob Killick

PS: For the fear of the Lord is still the beginning.

••

Vol. 38, No. 24, Sunday, 13 June 1993

Non–Biblical Christian Quotes
"You'll get yours later, Alice"

I'll concede that when this threatened judgement-to-come was spoken in the old TV sit-com *The Honeymooners,* there was not Christian context, but …

Last week we tripped over the theology of the fear of the Lord. Until quite recently—in year terms—the church held out the fear of judgement to come. This has acceptable antecedents. In Acts 24:25, Paul spoke to Felix about faith in Jesus Christ—righteousness, self-control, and the judgement to come. "Felix trembled with fear!" Jesus Himself left us the simple command: "Fear Him (God who is able to destroy both soul and body in hell" (Matt. 10:28), or in Luke 12:5: 'But I (Jesus) will forewarn you whom you shall fear. Fear Him who after He has killed has power to cast into hell; yes I say unto you, Fear Him!"

Last week I queried how the fear of the Lord can enter my life. No person simply duplicates another person's experience. The two thieves were both dying on their crosses; one railed on Jesus, but the other rebuked his compatriot, "Don't you fear God seeing you have received the same sentence" (Luke 23:40). One hung on the cross with the fear of the Lord in his heart, and Jesus could exclaim, "Today you will be with Me in paradise" (Luke 24:43).

No, I am still struggling on how the fear of the Lord impacts my life. I am commanded, "you call Him Father, when you pray to God, who judges all people by the same standard according to what each one has done; so then, spend the rest of your lives here on earth in fear of Him (1 Peter 1:17), or would it fit us better if we took the translation as "reverence," or Peter again says (1 Peter 2:17), "Respect everyone, love your fellow-believers, Fear God and respect the Emperor." Proverbs 1:24–33) provides a frightening glimpse of those who do not choose the fear of the Lord. (Nine verses for you to read.)

I command, therefore, I obey. I can choose, but how will it be evident in my life?

Bob Killick

PS: The fear of the Lord still remains at the beginning.

Vol. 38, No. 25, Sunday, 20 June 1993

Non-Biblical Christian Quotes (4)
("May fortune favour the foolish")

I often jot comments down believing one day they will be good for an Editorial. This is a fine system until, when I extracted the above, I can't remember the source or even whether it was from a book or a film.

With the best will in the world, my best remembrance would be one of the latter *Star Trek* movies, but not to worry, our heroes were ready to go into an impossible situation such that only the foolhardy or foolish would attempt. Yes, we all want fortune (Christian translation: Goodness and Mercy Psalm 23:6) to favour our ventures, whilst in the more cultural words of today: We want success to attend us.

I, therefore, reacted a trifle negatively the other day when I was reminded that when Paul had his successful ministry in Ephesus, he could claim in Acts 20:31, "I never stopped warning each of you night and day with tears." From being reminded that I certainly lack spiritual success, I was told that *our* problem, for the whole church was included, was that for starters, we lacked tears.

But Bob wishing to justify himself (Luke 10:29)said, "but we do want to see results for our labours!" Perhaps I am not of the heroic mould, but I nevertheless believe that I am part of the heroic church militant. Like an army, like a body, like the farmer (1 Cor. 3:6–7), there are those who cultivate, those who sow, those who reap, but it is still God that gives the increase. There will always be those who sow with tears and reap with joy (Psalm 126:5). Perhaps more the pity that most of us just cultivate.

And our foolishness is certainly not to be the plaintive cry of Saul in 1 Samuel 26:21, who looked back on his life and exclaimed, "I have played the fool." No, we are to link in with God with the message of the cross: "foolishness to those who are perishing, but to us who are being saved it is the power of God" (1 Cor. 1:18–25).

Bob Killick

PS: For the foolishness of God is still wiser.

••

Vol. 38, No. 26, Sunday, 27 June 1993

Non-Biblical Christian Quotes (5)
"Angels and Ministers of grace protect us"

The message came over the radio to flee from the coming flood! To his neighbours' entreaties, the Christian replied that God would look after him. As the water lapped the table, those in the boat begged him to jump aboard. "No," he said. "God will look after me." The helicopter crew begged him to be winched up as the water lapped the roof, but the offer was declined for God would look after him.

The last glimpse was the man standing in heaven complaining to God why he had not been protected? God simply replied, "I spoke through the radio, I sent the boat and the helicopter. What more did you want?"

Which leaves us with the question, how do Angels and ministers of grace protect us?

There is no doubt that they do look after us. We read in Hebrews 1:14, "Are not all angels ministering spirits sent to serve those who will inherit salvation?" So the first problem is that they are of spirit and thus invisible, but I can be made visible. In the account of Balaam (Num. 5:22), his ass had seen the angel but, "then the Lord opened the eyes of Balaam and he saw the Angel of the Lord standing in the way and his sword drawn in his hand and Balaam bowed down his head and fell flat on his face (Num. 5:31). See also the story of Elisha in 2 Kings 6:14–17).

No, I have not had my eyes opened that I can "see" the angels, but I still sing with surety:

> The hosts of God encamp around
> The dwellings of the just
> Protection He affords to all
> Who make His name their trust.

Our Christian at the start probably fell into the same trap that Satan tried on Jesus: "If you are the Son of God throw yourself from the temple, for Scripture says: He will put His angels in charge of you and they will support you in their arms for fear you should strike your foot against a stone" (Matt. 4:5–6). God has His angels to protect. But then we must never, never, never presume. Jesus answered Satan, "Scripture again says, 'You a not to put the Lord your God to the test'" (Matt. 4:7).

Bob Killick

PS: We do the exams, not God.

....

CHAPTER 4

Ain't She Sweet?

Just cast an eye in her direction
Oh me, oh my, ain't that perfection?
—Song from the Roaring Twenties *Ain't She Sweet?* 1927

As Yum-Yum departs, Ko-Ko reflects:
There she goes! To think how entirely my future
happiness is wrapped up in that little parcel!
(From Gilbert and Sullivan, *The Mikado*, 1885)

The first three chapters recounted Judy's early life amongst many, education, sport, music (including voice, dance, and piano), in the workforce, and marriage by the age of twenty. During the same time these talents were being honed, her gene pool was consolidating her natural expertise and special abilities. However, Judy's greatest gifts are not just limited to skills and aptitudes but matters of character and personality.

This chapter has to start with her parents, Malcolm Gillies and Freda Gillies (nee McFadzean) for they were the providers of her immediate gene pool that made her the complete parcel. Indeed, Mal and Freda were certainly characters in their own ways with much to pass on.

Malcolm McPherson Gillies—Judy's Father

Judy's father, Malcolm McPherson Gillies, was born March 17, 1907, at Orange Base Hospital. He was the fifth of six children of John and Lily Gillies. For no knowledge to the opposite, he had an uneventful childhood and attended Orange Primary School and Orange High School.

Below is the only photo of fifteen-year-old Mal. His teacher was Mr A. B. Walsh, who is wearing the bow tie.

Mal at fifteen years, centre row, second from right.

The only work he had in his early years was in his father's men's clothing store in Summer Street, Orange.

He joined the AMP Society in the late-1930s, and his life story splits between the next few paragraphs and the section highlighting his married life with Freda.

Attributed to the mother's influence, the Gillies family had been raised as Plymouth Brethren, shortened to the Plyms. However, in the middle years, three of the siblings—Mal, Fred, and Lil—left that group to go their own ways. Mal still rankled under the surface from some of the family experiences surrounding that departure. This came out when Judy had become a Christian, and she and I were in courting mode. Mal expressed his extreme concern that "Judy and Bob might become like the Plyms." We didn't.

Compared with Freda, Mal was a relatively quiet man, but he did go into the Orange amateur theatricals. He had a genetic heart problem that ran through the Gillies family, and he suffered a heart attack at age sixty-three. Freda was able to locate a unit in 1971. It had a lift and otherwise flat walking from the Camelot block of units into Manly. This seven-story building had replaced The Crescent Ballroom, where Judy and I had our wedding reception ten years earlier.

Mal's health continued to deteriorate, resulting in a major operation on his abdominal aorta at the Royal North Shore Hospital in 1974. This was followed in 1975 by a coronary occlusion. He was treated at Manly Hospital and subsequently admitted to Royal North Shore Hospital in 1976, where he died in September. One of our all-pervading memories of Mal was him sitting in a rocking chair facing the beautiful Sydney Harbour. His modus operandi was to start the day reading through the classified columns of the "Births, Deaths, and Marriages" in the *Sydney Morning Herald*. It was his guide to new contacts.

Mal Gillies, Judy's father.

The newspaper notification of Mal's passing read:

GILLIES: Malcolm McPherson, -
November 15, 1976, at hospital late of Manly,
Dearly loved husband of Freda, loved father and father-in-law
of Judith and Robert, John and Fay and fond
grandfather of their children.

The following brief eulogy was in the February 1977 issue of *Bowls in New South Wales*" in "Departed Bowlers" from the Manly Club.

> Mal Gillies joined the club in 1961 and served it with distinction. A good bowler and a good administrator, he was on committee for a number of years and was also a selector. Unfortunately, he, too, suffered ill-health in recent years and while he was able to continue as a player, he had to relinquish participation in club administration. But he was a good counsellor for new members, a role which befitted his sincere interest in the game.

Freda Sidney Gillies (nee McFadzean)—Judy's Mother

Freda was born on January 12, 1909, at Studleigh, O'Connor Street, Haberfield, Sydney, NSW, and for all her life, even to the old-age home, she was known for her energy and effervescence. In those early days in Orange, she was what used to be called "a real goer" or "a real hard case." That is, someone incorrigible with their own style of living.

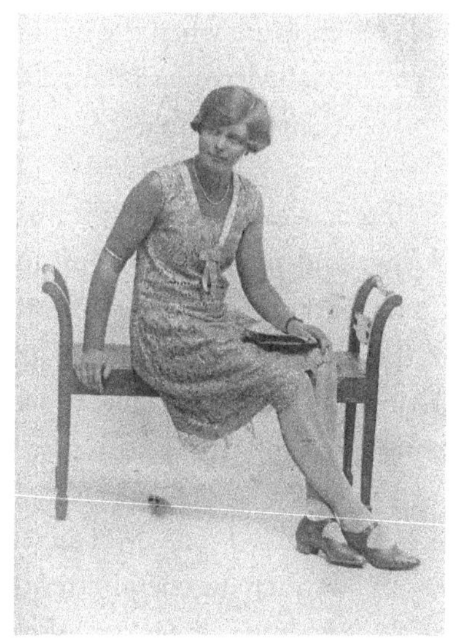

Freda at seventeen.

To this day, Judy remembers when as a child she watched the guests arrive at their home in their fancy dress finery. There were squeals of shocked amazement once when Freda greeted the guests dressed with two saucepan lids covering the strategic chest-high equipment and one fig leaf covering the nether region. One could almost joke that it was "Show Time." Please do not be surprised that no photos exist of that episode.

Freda's training to be in front of an audience was well established before her teens as two shows were reported when she was ten years old. The *Orange Leader* newspaper reported on June 18, 1919:

> Miss Iris Flower's Recital
>
> For her recital of "Dadsy and Babsy" with pianoforte accompaniment by Miss Gladys Mackenzie, little Miss Freda McFadzean received tumultuous applause and was also rewarded with a floral tribute.

Four months later, the indefatigable *Orange Leader* (October 17, 1919) provided:

> Convent Juvenile Ball
>
> The grand march, in which over 200 children participated, was a sight well worth seeing, and the judging of the fancy costumes, though difficult was received with well-merited applause when the winners were announced: … and Freda McFadzean as "Baby Doll." They all looked charming in their costumes.

Freda was also known for her sporting prowess, particularly in tennis, skiing, and in lawn bowling in her later years. She was a typist in the Orange branch of the New South Wales Lands Department and a member of their tennis team, which would play competitive tennis on the Miloton Tennis Courts in Brisbane. During her visit there in April 1935, the *Herald* reported as follows:

> Young Freda McFadzean, from Orange, was one who attracted general attention. A cousin of the late Daphne Akhurst, she is remarkably like her except for her fair hair, and one could see in Freda the same charm that won all hearts when Daphne was playing.

Freda would save up all year so she could holiday at Kosciusko each winter. She was a lady who somehow kept ending up in the social sections of the newspapers as the following clipping shows:

> The Misses Freda McFadzean and Jean Dumont, of Orange arrived in Kosciusko a couple of weeks ago for the winter sports. They found snow conditions good, and there was also skating on the lake in front of the hotel and on the courtyard rink. During their visit, these ladies spent a night at the chalet at Charlotte Pass, the journey of 22 miles being made on skis … On Friday night a fancy dress ball was held at the Hotel Kosciusko, the prize for the best dressed lady being awarded to Miss McFadzean. She represented "Dolly Varden" and was undoubtedly the sweetest character among a great variety of excellent costumes."

Freda in a fancy dress.

Dolly Varden is generally understood to mean a brightly patterned, usually flowered dress with a polonaise overskirt gathered up and draped over a separate underskirt. It comes from the character from Charles Dickens's 1839 historical novel *Barnaby Rudge*.

Freda died on December 15, 1996, in Mulgrave, a south-eastern suburb of Melbourne.

The Freda-Mal Marriage Union

Nothing is known of Freda and Mal's courtship. It best could be described as an attraction of opposites. They were both in Orange's amateur plays and musicals. Freda always claimed that, as well as her own, she had to learn Mal's lines so she could keep prompting him. Freda was the extrovert and all of life was showtime. When at forty-seven years old she became a Christian, Mal could only comment, "It's only an act!" It wasn't. Judy's brother, John, was recently reviewing the family past and Freda and Mal's stormy relationship. But when Freda became a Christian, peace settled over the household.

On the night before her marriage, Freda was in her room crying, "I don't want to get married. I don't want to get married!"

Her mother, Alice, stomped in, "Of course you do, Freda. Don't be silly!" And she did!

Judy's parents were married on Thursday, November 14, 1935, at the Orange Presbyterian Church. The three bridesmaids in attendance were Hazel and Nancy, Freda's sisters, and the adopted sister, Gwen, with two young teenagers carrying the bridal train and the seven-year-old flower girl who led the procession. Fred Gillies, Mal's younger brother, was the best man and two friends were groomsmen.

The two local papers got carried away, extracts of which follow.

Wedding: Gillies-McFadzean

> It was in a beautiful setting on Thursday evening, just as the sun was sinking at the close of a glorious day, and in surroundings made still more beautiful by the decorations in the Church that a crowded gathering witnessed one of the prettiest weddings that has taken place in Orange for some considerable time, and an event that had created more than ordinary interest because of the extreme popularity of the contracting parties ... The bride, leaning on the arm of her father, looked radiant as she entered the Church ... Her magnificent veil of tulle was loaned by Mrs Erby, the wife of Dr Erby, whose sister Miss Daphne Akhurst wore at her wedding ... Mr. and Mrs. Gillies left by car for Sydney amidst crowds of friends and well-wishers, and on Friday will join the Strathnaven on route for New Zealand, where their honeymoon will be spent. A large number of presents, including cheques, were on view at the home of the bride.

A newspaper cutting from the *Orange Advocate*, January 1936, includes a report on the first meeting Freda and Mal attended on their return from their honeymoon. It was the "Apex Ladies' Night" in the form of a dinner, musical, and elocutionary entertainment and dance. It was one of the brightest and versatile functions organised by the club wherein, "in a humorous elocutionary item, which has previously won for her recognition in Orange, Mrs. Gillies provided what could be described as one of the gems of the entertainment." This was the one elocutionary item that truly became Freda's party piece over all the years. Its title was "A Pleasant Half-Hour at the Beach," also known as "Aggie at the Beach."

The cutting continued:

> Apexian Mac Gillies, director of music, led the company in community singing, the number being that novelty made by Billy Cotton and his band "I Can't Dance, Got Ants in My Pants." Part singing, in which members and guests participated, was wholly enjoyable, and certainly responsible for much brightness. Prior to this, Apexians Mac Gillies and Cyril Blowes sang a duet, which was cheered to the echo. …
>
> "We must thank Mrs Mac Gillies," said the President. "We realise now that Mac is married, he will become all the keener about Apex, and attend all the dinners, board meetings, etc." (Laughter.) He said that members of the Orange Apex Club were glad to be among those to honour one of the most popular members of the local organisation and his charming wife, who had always been to the fore in assisting any movement put forward by Apex in Orange. He was privileged to make them a presentation—a beautiful coloured glass bowl—on behalf of Apexians. Apexian Gillies responded saying that the gift would be one of the most cherished in their home, because it would remind them of the kindly thought of his colleagues in Apex.
>
> A motion was then carried that as the newly married Apexian of Orange, Mac Gillies should sing a song. He

obliged with a rendition of one of Richard Tauber's recent musical successes.

Already noted above for his singing, Mal also enjoyed playing the harmonica. When the family settled into their own home, a "bitsa" dog was acquired called Dinky. Without pedigree, there were no problems. It didn't get sick, it ate the leftover scraps, and was impervious to the bush ticks. Its only problem was that it would accompany Mal's harmonica playing with mournful howling. There was also one other problem that comes to mind in that the dog would attack the author when he called on Judy to go courting. Dinky was obviously not sane.

Mal was doing well in the AMP Society, and the local paper reported on May 13, 1940, "Mr Gillies is leaving next Monday for Newcastle having been promoted by the directors of the AMP Society." The invitation to their farewell party invitation ran:

YOU ARE INVITED TO
BLOW ALONG TO

A WET FAREWELL

TO

FREDA AND MAC GILLIES

AT THE BLUE ROOM

ON THURSDAY, 9 MAY 1940

LADS 5/- DON'T LET US DOWN

DAMAGE RING 467

LASSIES 3/- AND LET'S KNOW

The paper on Monday, May 13, 1940, thence reported: "More than 100 attended the farewell party given to Mr. and Mrs. Mac Gillies ... The guests of honour were presented with a traymobile."

Newcastle did not last long when Mal joined the war effort. This was pleasing to Freda as she particularly did not like the larger, sooty, steel city after being the "Queen of the Ball" in Orange's social world where she knew everyone, and everyone knew her. She returned to live in Orange for the next three-plus years at 110 Moulder Street. Mal's, enlistment number NX 110274, on March 4, 1942, was a member of the Citizen Military

Forces and Australian Imperial Force. He served on continuous full-time war service for 1,194 days.

He was discharged on June 9, 1945, with the rank of sergeant from the 17 Aust. Supply Depot Company. He had spent most of his time in Tenterfield. When he was discharged, he had an ulcer condition for which he received a disability pension. After Mal's death, the payments continued to Freda until her death and were affectionately known as "Mal's stomach money."

Whatever Mal's thoughts may have been for future employment, a return to the menswear shop was not on the cards. John, his father, sold the Orange menswear business due to his onset of blindness. This forced their return to Sydney and the maelstrom of finding accommodation to rent under the Landlord and Tennant Act. It was most fortunate that Freda's brother-in-law, Harry Beveridge, was moving out of their rented cottage to take up the position of accountant of the Commonwealth Bank at Bellingen NSW. Rather than Harry turning up to pay the monthly rent, it was Mal with the payment, which was received by the real estate agent, which gave the Gillies family the right to remain in 25 Wood Street, Chatswood. This was the end of life-in-Orange. The local newspaper reported the event in the Saturday paper of May 11, 1946:

> Mr and Mrs Mac Gillies, with their two children, Judy and John, returned to Sydney last week to make their home in Chatswood, after being the guests of Mrs Gillies' parents of 66 Kite Street. Mr Gillies was for some time with the fighting forces. Prior to leaving they were entertained by "their large circle of friends."

"Their large circle of friends" really says it all for Freda was not at all enamoured with the Chatswood out-of-the-way Wood Street. And having no friends, she labelled the area "Gillies Gully." The problem of finding friends in town seems to be the curse of busyness, and this was even picked up by "Banjo" Paterson in 1889 in his poem "Clancy of the Overflow." It is one of Banjo's best-known works and offers a romantic view of rural life whilst in town he could only see:

And the hurrying people daunt me, and their pallid faces haunt me
As they shoulder one another in their rush and nervous haste,
With their eager eyes and greedy, and their stunted forms and weedy,
For townsfolk have no time to grow, they have no time to waste.

The big change for the family was the purchase of a block of land at 20 Plant Street, Seaforth, to build their own home. This story is told in chapter 3.

Mal had returned to Sydney to become a representative for the AMP Society, where he remained for the rest of his working life. His professional breakthrough to become a millionaire-salesman was to organize the life insurance policies of Ken Rosewall and Lew Hoad, two of Australia's greatest tennis players. They were known as the "golden twins of tennis." For a couple of years after that coup, tickets used to come the family's way for them to be spectators at Sydney's White City tennis courts.

To expand his retirement funds, Mal built *Seillig* (Gillies backwards), a block of units at 12 Fairlight Street, Manly. It had a ground floor and two stories. Freda and Mal lived on the top floor. This was not appreciated by Freda, having to lug the groceries up two flights of stairs.

Mal was a wealth creator and had a strong work ethic with an overriding desire that he and his Freda could retire without expecting the government pension. In those days, to be on the old age pension was considered to have been a business failure in life.

Aspects of the Honing of Judy's DNA

It was appropriate to have lingered with Judy's parents' shenanigans for the richness there reflects much of Judy's DNA-derived personality with a few examples following.

Ever the Life of the Party

That Judy thrives in the company of other people and enjoys being the life of the party is not unknown to those fortunate enough to experience the full extent of her hospitality. I am reminded in this regard of the time forty or so years ago when we had just arrived home from a family beach holiday in Merimbula southern NSW. It was a seven-hour drive, and we were recovering with a cup of tea out the back of our house with Judy declaring that she had "had it!" and wanted nothing more than to fall asleep. Of course, her views changed the instant one of her good friends from round the corner dropped by, and for the next hour, conversation failed to cease. And the appropriate word here is "conversation." When Judy is around, there is no shortage of conversation, and if you want any part in it, you've got to be good to get in. It is a fact of life that she has an antipathy to silence, which speaks to her warmth, enthusiasm, and love of people.

Frugality

Judy well remembers two events. The first was as part of the Apexians Association's activities. Hospitality was offered to those visiting from overseas, and Mal was to look after Archibald from Scotland. Freda had quietly drawn Judy and John aside and told them clearly that she did not want them sniggering at Archibald's name when they were introduced to him. All went smoothly until the bread, butter, and strawberry jam were tabled. With shock and incredulity, Judy and John gasped, "Strawberry jam!" It had never been part of the menu for it was exotic and certainly too costly to be part of the family menu. Living was frugal.

The second time was when Judy's mum blew a fuse and told Mal she was "going on strike" and would not be getting out of bed until he increased the housekeeping allowance! "You have no idea, Mal, how food prices have gone up!" John and Judy never learned how much more she received, but then she never knew how much Mal earned.

Frugality has remained Judy's watchword during her life. Tales abound of husbands who feel they would be unwise to provide their wives with a credit card. The reverse can also be true. This has never been a problem with Judy. She always had a credit card.

I Hear What You're Saying

That being said, another mark of Judy's character is her listening ear and her extraordinary ability to empathise. In contrast to the author, who has the patience for about three seconds of empathetic listening before launching into providing instruction or leaning in and lending a proffered handkerchief, Judy's gift in this area shines a bright light on the shortcomings of said author. Far from offering a lowly sympathetic handkerchief in place of understanding, Judy's patience, compassion, and unceasing inclination towards prayer in those situations that require an empathetic ear, mark her as a woman who not only relishes the company of others but who would see the success, comfort, and happiness of those around her. As Rick Warren has pertinently articulated, "You see pain with your eyes but sympathise with your ears. Sometimes the greatest way to serve someone is just by listening." Behind every need is a story, and Judy has always had an ear for other people's stories.

Common Sense/Wisdom

Early in our marriage, Judy began the long, slow process of teaching me many of the basic lessons of life that I was not to forget. One of the key ones required maximum input, and as I was going out to work each morning, she would grab me by the lapels, shake me like a wet rat, and say, "Remember, all wisdom does not lie with Bob Killick!"

Another time was when we were selling the Richmond property and buying Henkel's factory at Coolaroo. The Richmond purchaser suggested we should leave the proceeds in a partnership and build together and, "we would earn more money" to share. Once again I went through the "shaken rat process," and Judy said, "You know how to make chemicals and sell chemicals. You know nothing about building twelve-storey buildings. Take the money and make it happen at Coolaroo! Remember, 'the cobbler should stick to his last.'" Best advice as the building project took thirteen years to complete, and the "increased" funds appear while it was all happening at Coolaroo!

Eve in the Garden

I would be remiss as husband and author if I did not, in this chapter on Judy's character, mention her pride of place and joy and talent she finds in her garden. This love and gift for gardening is certainly one that must begin at least in the memories of her grandfather, Frederick Lamont McFadzean, known as Pop (from the cartoon "Popeye the Sailor"). He was a notably enthusiastic gardener and is fondly remembered for his "Sulphur

Queen" Dahlias. If her love for her garden was to be surmised in one word, it would be *pining*, as whenever we are away for any length of time, the thing that Judy pines over most of all is to return and take an educated guess at how many roses alone she managed to install in the space of a rather limited suburban garden (not to mention the countless other flowers and plants that augment our humble abode). Seventy would not be too generous an estimate. After a pruning, she is likely to get forty new roses and has to give many of them away as we simply do not have the space.

Whilst roses are certainly a favourite with Judy, and a flower for which she is well known, her talent for gardening is not limited to the aesthetic or the sheer number and variety of plants she grows. Her garden also showcases her perseverance, ingenuity, and ability to adapt as in gardening, success is not least owed to one's capacity and inclination to learn through a process of trial and error. One such memorable example that reveals Judy's talent as a gardener happy to adapt to further gardening success is when she swapped roses for geraniums.

Our house lies at the end of a street. The opposite end backs onto the local primary school our children attended. The concrete garden wall that separates our home from the footpath was just wide enough for the schoolchildren to walk on. In an effort to put an end to the wall-walking, Judy had a stroke of genius and made a garden along the wall, where she planted roses in the garden. The thorns did deter the wall-walkers and provided an attractive line of roses. Judy decided to extend the line and planted six lovely freshly struck roses. One night shortly after, someone came by and purloined the lot. Within the week, Judy had planted another six roses, and the roses were again stolen overnight. The next day, geraniums replaced the roses, and to this day, they have not been stolen. Thus ends the fiasco of the front garden wall.

Thankfulness

Perhaps the most poignant double questions by Jesus in scripture follow the healing of the ten lepers. The questions were simplicity in themselves: "Were there not ten cleansed? Where are the other nine?" The question that comes back to ourselves is simply how thankful we are even over small matters of life.

If we got good seats at the theatre, Judy would turn to me and declare, "Bob, you couldn't have chosen better." Such a sentiment works even better with a final reflection on Judy, my wife of noble character. Not a day goes by when I cannot but say to myself regarding my wife: "Bob, you couldn't have chosen better."

God Always Guides His People

By this stage of my life, the teachings of the Christian faith that formed the basis of our lives' primary purpose were making us sensitive to doing God's will. At one extreme, the teaching emphasised that only by laying down all one's desires on the "altar of sacrifice" could we be really blessed as disciples of Jesus. At the other extreme, Augustine of Hippo's thesis was, "Love God and do what you like." Having earned my PhD and with Judy as my wife, it was time to launch into the very competitive business world to find a job where God wanted us to be. Some people venture that Christianity is for lily-livered weaklings, but far from being a crutch, Christianity was to prove to be the compass that enabled Judy and I to launch into the real marketplace and embrace whatever God's adventure for us.

Part of our experience over the years has been in the production and direction of church concerts and shows. As the director of a show, I learned the importance of people doing what they were directed to do. This became a practical application to our lives in recognition that God was in control. He was the prime mover, the top director. It gave us comfort to know that He does all things well, and our job was to look out for His direction. There were times when matters did not seem to be going as we would want, yet afterward, we were able to look back and see that God had guided us towards a better outcome than we would have chosen for ourselves. It reminded us particularly of the biblical story of Joseph when he said to his brothers, "You determined it for evil but God worked it for good" (Genesis 50:20).

CHAPTER 5

Scotland the Brave

Every (family) tree has some "sap" in it.

—Notebook ex Zazzle.com

There were certainly some characters in the early days.

—W. Alexander Brown 1952–

It is one thing to have an appreciation of the role of genes in heredity, but there are also the almost inexplicable permutations and combinations of life. The chief of these is the union of the parents who found each other in the appropriate social milieu, in the same location, at the right children-bearing ages so they could meet, fall in love, marry, and have a child. Hello, Judy!

The parents, ah yes, the parents. Both were characters in their own rights, and one can only say that Judy's mum, Freda, was a "real hard case." Mal and Freda were nitpicked in chapter 4.

But now for the first question: "Why was Australia going to be graced by their presence?"

Why Australia?

It is a big world, yet Judy's forebears did find Australia rather than, for example, Canada or America. The following 1992 Editorial provides a risible reason.

Vol. 35, No. 38, Sunday, 20 September 1992

Esoteric Non-Biblical Quotes (3)
("I like beachfront property, I'll take Australia.")

Yes, I can give you a clue that this quote is from the movies. Any ideas? No? Well, it is tucked into the *Superman* series within which the three criminals from Krypton are negotiating with that evil genius, that greatest criminal mind of his time, that fiendishly gifted Lex Luthor, for the whereabouts of Superman. But the Krypton men are realists and asked, "But what payment would you want from us if you give us this information?"

Lex Luthor replied, "I like beachfront property, I'll take Australia!"

I'm not certain whether we have been undersold or overvalued.

Land and its ownership, or lack of it, not only pervades scripture but to this day, most conflicts and wars are caused by it. From God's promise to Abram that "to your children I will give this land" (Gen. 12:7), Abraham's children, Jew (from Jacob) and Arab (from Esau), still fight for the spoils today.

For the Christian, however, there has never been a promise of land. To be a kingdom child, the start of our aspirations is that the "King is not of this world, otherwise my servants would fight" (John 18:36). No, we don't fight for land, but then the New Testament does not indicate that it is neither sinful nor evil to own land. It is just not an issue unless it becomes an obsessive chase. Or perhaps we don't chase for it but sit and covet, which is idol worship (Col. 3:5).

I don't know, but I don't think that any of us really want to gain the whole world. I mean, who would want to try and run the mess? For many, there remains the possible "Australian dream" of our own house on its quarter acre in the suburbs. If we have our house and live godly lives with contentment, it is great gain (1 Tim. 6:9). If we don't own our own property, the Bible still says to live godly lives with contentment as it is great gain for we are ever reminded that we brought nothing into this world, and we are certainly not going to take anything out. No, Paul continues in 1 Timothy 6:11 that our pursuit in life is to follow after righteousness, godliness, faith, love, patience, and meekness. Or as Jesus summarised, "Seek first the Kingdom and all the other baggage gets thrown in behind" (Matt. 6:33).

Bob Killick

PS: For those with faint hearts who don't watch *Superman* movies, Lex Luthor didn't get his beachfront property, and the naughty men got their just deserts.

....

For the record, the following table provides Judy's first antecedents' arrivals for each grandparental line. The choice of country appears to have depended on the salesmanship of those promoting the future country as described for Donald Gillies in chapter 1. The final driving forces were the escape from poverty or to simply achieve a better life.

First Arrivals in Australia of Judy's Antecedents

Judy's Grandparents	Judy's First Ancestors in Australia	Boat	Arrival Date
Paternal			
John Gillies	John's grandfather, Donald, was forty-two on arrival from the Isle of Skye, Scotland.	*Midlothian*	**1837** December 12
Lily Anderson Beveridge	Lily was six on arrival from Dumferline, Scotland, with her father, Laurence Beveridge.	*Loch Garry*	**1880** September 26
Maternal			
Frederick Lamont McFadzean	Frederick's grandfather, Mathew McFadzean came from Ayrshire, Scotland.	Not known	**1860** Not known
Alice Edith Akhurst	Alice's grandfather, William Mower Akhurst came from London.	*Posthumous*	**1849** June 20

Amongst Judy's forebears there were no convicts but only free settlers fleeing poverty and looking to find a better life. The four bloodlines were now in Australia, three-fourths coming from Scotland and the other fourth from England. Some minor German heredity was introduced into the English Akhurst line when Sidney Philip, William Mower's son, married Alice Kitz, whose parents came from Hanau as mentioned in chapter 6.

There is a slight digression to consider how Blackmans Swamp Creek became the city of Orange.

Some Early Colonial History

Whilst Australia's founding was on January 26, 1788, Sydney's expansion was limited for the next twenty-five years by the lack of agricultural land. With what they had, the farmers preferred to raise sheep and cattle rather than grow barley. This lack was overcome in one twenty-one-day period, May 11 to June 6, 1813. It was the time for the crossing of the Blue Mountains, which had previously confined the fledgling colony to the coastal fringe. The early attempts to cross were along the river valleys, but with the forbidding maze of sandstone bluffs, deep gorges, and dense bush, they were considered impassable. The explorers Blaxland, Lawson, and Wentworth's success came by following the mountain ridges. The party first saw the plains beyond the mountains from Mount York and later from Mount Blaxland, where Lawson wrote in his journal, "the best watered country of any I have seen in the colony."

Governor Lachlan Macquarie, who was probably one of the best governors Australia has had, was proactive. Within five months, on November 13, he sent G. W. Evans, the surveyor general, to follow the explorers' route and then go west to look at the unknown land. Evans reached the end point of the previous exploration on November 26. He scouted for the next seven weeks, and by December 9, they were at the present site of Bathurst. Moving south-west, Evans sighted, "high distant mountains," which we now know would include Mount Canobolas, the dominating mountain of Blackman's Swamp Creek. Ever indefatigable, Governor Macquarie and his wife left Sydney on April 25, 1815, crossing the Blue Mountains on the road he ordered built and continuing west to their namesake river. Over a week they decided on a suitable site for a town they named Bathurst. This became the jumping-off point for agriculture and continuing exploration.

Ancestral Village

If we were in the United States looking into the background of Judy's ancestral village, I am sure we would be hoping to get something exotic like Dead Man's Gulch Village. I never thought Australia would start with something memorable, but surprise! Judy's ancestral village started out as Blackman's Swamp Creek.

Initially, a convict settlement was established in 1822 at Blackman's Swamp and named after an explorer of the district, James Blackman. By 1829, the name of Orange was allocated on a plan as a village reserve. The name was chosen as an honour to the prince of Orange, who became the king of Holland in 1840. However, the area reserved for a village had, by late 1829, immigrant graziers encroaching over it.

By 1844, it was necessary to settle on the location of a village. The choice fell among Blackman's Swamp, Frederick's Valley, and Pretty Plains. Blackman's Swamp was chosen. In 1846, it was proclaimed a village named Orange. There was an early fillip to the village with the discovery of gold in 1851 at the nearby hamlet of Ophir, eighteen kilometres distant, and Orange joined the Australian gold rush. With additional finds in nearby areas, particularly Lucknow, the establishment of Orange as a central trading centre for the gold was soon established. It was Ophir that had the honour of introducing the words *digger* and *diggings* into the Australian lexicon, which were used for and by Australians in the First World War.

Horticulture was soon established, and the district became known as a major producer of apples, pears, and cherries. Judy well remembers as a child being swept along in the annual, springtime Cherry Blossom Parade in the main street of the city.

There are thousands of books, monographs, scientific papers, and so on that set out to provide an understanding of the mysteries of character. Who, in the fullest sense, is Judy, and how did she get to be?

It would appear persistence is the trait that hides behind the successful activity of passing down a person's heredity. It is the genes—the basic physical units of heredity in our bodies—that have persistence in "heaps," 100 per cent having been carried forward from our earliest ancestors in different amounts and sometimes with slight changes (mutations).

Is It Heredity, Genetics, or DNA?

As her biographer, my aim is to provide a written picture of Judy as a physical person and her personality. To obtain some understanding, it is interesting to consider the genes handed down by her forebears.

Heredity is readily seen in the human body through observable traits such as height, build, eye colour, skin colour, and even a tendency toward some types of baldness. This body heredity can't be affected by nurture! Judy is short in frame, as was her father and grandfather, olive skin and hearing problems from her mother, blue eyes from both parents, and so on. She is certainly a chip off the old blocks.

It is the unobservable traits that cause much discussion. Some geneticists are convinced that many personality traits and behaviours are passed down through the generations not by one but by groups or pools of genes. These include anger, musical talent, and laziness. On the other hand, it is also claimed that these genes only give the *potential* for the development of the traits depending on external factors—such as the environment, lifestyle, and experiences—that finally produce the person's temperament. At one extreme, there are people who are stale, stodgy, stay-at-home idlers. At the other are those who are fresh, interesting, and adventuring opportunists. All the world's people lie somewhere across the spectrum.

A List of Characters

Each of Judy's four ancestral bloodlines based on her grandparents contained at least one character who stands out from the rest. Notwithstanding the circumstances of their lives, they are not equal in the level of their largeness of life.

From Judy's grandfather's male line (John Gillies), there were three: Don Gillies—"The Immigrants from the Misty Isle"; Malcolm Gillies—"The Early Capitalist"; and grandfather John Gillies himself—"Business Entrepreneur."

From Judy's grandfather's female line (Lily Anderson Beveridge), there was Lily herself—"The Orphan."

From Judy's grandmother's male line (Frederick Lamont McFadzean), there was Frederick himself—"There's Gold in Them Thar Hills."

Back in Judy's grandmother's female line of Alice Edith Akhurst, there had been William Mower Akhurst—"A Bohemian Down Under" and Alice Kitz—"The Germanic Link."

This chapter follows Judy's grandfather's male line.

Judy's Father's Antecedents: Grandfather's Line

Earliest of the Gillies

"Gillies" is a long-established Scottish name deriving from the Gaelic words *gille lose*, which means "servant of Jesus." The Gillies clan claims its descent from the Dalriada kingdom located on the Scottish west coast. This Gaelic kingdom started in Northern Ireland and soon included the Inner Hebrides and Argyllshire. It received extensive immigration from the Irish. Whilst the kingdom was at its zenith in AD 500, it ultimately lost its political identity after the Viking invasions early in the ninth century. After much fighting between the Dalriadas to the west and the Picts to the east, the two groups united under Kenneth I, also called Kenneth MacAlpin, the first king of Scots and Picts. Thereafter, the territory was known as Scotland. He died about AD 858.

The first written references, with variable spelling, to the Gillies name were in Lothian County, which abuts Edinburgh to the west. There, in about 1128, a member of the Gillise family was a witness to the charter by King David I to the Abbey of Holyrood. In 1160, Vhtred Gilise inherited the estates in Lothian, and in 1164, M. filius Gilise witnessed a confirmation charter of Malcolm IV to the Abbey of Scone.

Don Gillies: "The Immigrants from the Misty Isle"

Poverty

Judy often says that she is glad that her forebears chose to leave Scotland for Australia. This is not saying that Scotland is not a nice place for a holiday, although it was not a tourist brochure that commented, two-thirds of the land is harsh, rocky, ill-drained, and swept by rain-bearing winds off the Atlantic Ocean. But emigration does not happen without strong driving forces behind the decision. Societal research has always noted that poverty was the main, traditional reason people left their home countries. An article in *The Sydney Herald* of 1842 on the impoverished immigrants stated:

> "They were totally unable to pay their own passage-money, and consequently were carried out at the expense of the

> colonial emigration fund. Many of them had no property whatever besides their clothes, and some had to be assisted even with clothing, before they could undertake the voyage ..." Quoting from several parishes—"The poor tenants are almost invariably under the necessity of having their cattle under the same roof with themselves, without partition, without division, and without a chimney; their houses are smoky and filthy in the extreme, and, having little either of night or day clothing, and their children nearly approaching to absolute nakedness, they are fully as much without cleanliness in their persons as they are in their houses. No people on earth live on more simple or scanty diet than those in this parish. The greater numbers of them subsist on potatoes of the worst kind, sometimes with, but oftener, without fish."

In the seventeenth century, the formation of a literate population resulted in five universities in a country of under a million people. In an underdeveloped Scottish economy, there was a shortage of middle-class jobs, but the canny Scots were soon found in Africa as missionaries and China and Japan as traders. For the impoverished Scot, however, Australia and New Zealand were seen as the lands of opportunity. By 1850, Scots made up a quarter of the population of New Zealand. Skye, along with Mull and the Long Island, became well known as a major source of immigrants, particularly as the Clearances took hold in the 1840s.

Sectarianism

Generally, sectarianism occurs when members of different denominations within a faith display prejudice and bigotry towards each other. Examples include the Sunni and Shania within Islam and Orthodox and Reform within Judaism. In Scotland, it was between the Scottish Protestants and the Irish Catholics. What also kept the situation on edge was during the times of high levels of Irish immigration into Scotland, the new arrivals were prepared to take less than the minimum wage. They were harassed in newspapers and regarded as drunks, lazy, uncivilized, and damaging to the moral character of Scottish society. As late as 1923, pamphlets such as *The Menace of the Irish Race to Our Scottish Nationality* were promulgated.

Meanwhile, a similar battle was raging in Australia with the Reverend John Dunmore Lang, an energetic young Presbyterian clergyman, at the helm. He arrived in NSW in 1822 and built the first Scots Church in Sydney (demolished in 1926). His main passion was to increase the level of Protestant Scottish immigration to address the imbalance of Irish Roman Catholics in the colony. He believed it was his destiny to be the one to save Australia from becoming an Irish Catholic country. Lang made nine trips to Scotland from NSW in order to arrange for the selection of suitable people. The result was that during the next three years, over four thousand Highlanders emigrated in eighteen ships.

Last Days on Scottish Soil

No specific records have been located of Judy's direct descendants before 1790. The Gillies name was not uncommon during that time and the following period in the region of Sleat, which was the home of the Lord McDonald, formally known as the "Lord of the Isles." Sleat has been called the "Garden of Skye." The Gillies intermarried with the McDonalds, McQueens, McGaskills, Nicholsons, and other proud Highland clans. As an example, there was the 1823 marriage of James Gillies to Rachel McDonald.

Donald and Margaret Gillies, who were to move to Australia, lived with his parents, James and Isabella Gillies, in a rented croft on the estate of the Lord McDonald of Sleat. A croft is an enclosed area of land, usually small, arable, and with a dwelling thereon. Don and Margaret were needed to help with the running of the farm and were, as yet, unable to rent a small croft of their own. There is reference to Margaret's mother, known as "Old Maggie."

The Good Ship *Midlothian*

Lang's fourth voyage to Scotland was the crucial one for Donald and Margaret Gillies and their family in that one of his two commissions was to bring back farm labourers with experience. In March 1837, an announcement was made from the pulpit of the Presbyterian Church at Kilmore in Sleat:

> My friends, following on the recent visit to our parish by our highly esteemed friend Doctor John Dunmore Lang, from Australia, I have to tell you that next week Doctor David Boyter will be present here in Sleat, to meet those of you who are anxious to migrate to the colonies. He will head a selection committee, of which I shall be one, to choose the most suitable migrants.

A few weeks later, Doctor Boyter stood in the church at Kilmore surveying the white faces, eyes fixed on bonneted women wrapped in plaid shawls, bearded shepherds with straggling locks, highland bonnets aslant, rough woven kilts. The faint smell of grime and poverty was in the air— a cow smell, an earth smell. They seemed the most spirited, as though they expected to hear something wonderful from him. This was followed by a medical examination and the sonorous words, "People of character are required."

Of course, they were chosen.

Their ship was the *Midlothian,* "a small barque of only 414 tons," and, "a bad sailing vessel, what mariners term a tub." The *Midlothian* departed on August 8, 1837, from the small port of Uig, in Loch Snizort on the north-west corner of the Isle of Skye, carrying 259 Highlanders or Gaels, all from the Isle of Skye. The voyage was 129 days long, travelling straight through to Sydney with the water and provisions having to last the whole trip. A 1911 article in the *Clarence and Richmond Examiner* suggests that the "fever" on board, including an outbreak of dysentery and typhus that killed thirty-six people was borne by starvation due to bad water and insufficient and bad rations. However, the ship had been well provisioned by the authorities, but the owners directed the captain and officers not to give out the provisions supplied for the emigrants, but to sell them at a profit when they reached Sydney, where food was scarce and dear. One of those who succumbed was a thirty-five-year-old John Gillies who, it was laconically stated in the log, "deceased in quarters." He left behind a wife (thirty-three) and six children; the youngest was just one year old. No link has been found between this John Gillies and Donald Gillies. John has simply become a statistic of the voyage.

The boat spent the last night in Jervis Bay and entered Sydney Heads the following day, December 12, 1837. After being cleared at anchor in Neutral Bay, it disembarked the passengers at Port Jackson on December 13, when they were taken to the immigration building, and a Gaelic service of thanksgiving was held for safe deliverance to their new home and the religious fervour that strongly marked the *Midlothian* immigrants. The "good" ship *Midlothian* had done its duty, although from all reports, the voyage from England was euphemistically, and perhaps better described as "a voyage from hell."

So, Donald and Margaret Gillies had brought their family of six to their new home. The family constituents are listed below, including an indication of the children's families in later years.

	Born	Died	Age on Arrival	
Donald	c.1795	1854	42	
Margaret	c. 1799	1877	38	
Mary*	1809	1829	*	*Deceased before *Midlothian* sailed.
John*	1811	1831	*	*Deceased before *Midlothian* sailed.
Jane	1818	1881	19	Married twice, had ten living children.
Donald	1821	1894	16	Had twelve living children.
Malcolm	1821	1907	16	Had eleven living children.
Anne	1823	1907	14	Married several times, had seven living children.
Hugh*	1829	1833	*	*Deceased before *Midlothian* sailed.
Christina	1829	1894	5	Had ten living children.
Catherine	1832	1889	3	Had eight living children.

Miller's Forest

The new immigrants immediately became the subject of controversy. They refused to be split up like the previous two government-assisted migrant shiploads, claiming that the government had promised to settle them as a community with their own minister who could speak Gaelic, only 20 per cent being able to speak English as a second language. The government decided that, although no such undertaking had been given, if any local landholder was willing to take them as a body, they would be given six months rations' from the Queen's stores and passage to the estate in question at the public's expense. John Dunmore Lang's brother Andrew was the only one willing to take them onto his 2,500-acre Dunmore estate, within two miles of the village of Morpeth from which there was daily communication by steamboats with the town of Sydney. The land was alluvial and of the "utmost fertility." The area slowly became known as the food bowl of Sydney.

Dunmore House, Paterson's River.
This 1937 watercolour by Robert Russell was undoubtedly built in a style to remember England.

Donald and family accepted the offer, and on January 23, 1838, along with thirty-two other families, or 154 passengers from the *Midlothian*, travelled to Dunmore on the Hunter River. The other families had taken other employment. The two steamers, the *Tamar* and the *Sophia Jane*, departed Sydney at 7 p.m. to arrive the next day at noon. The settlement employment terms as tenants were, "Small farms, of from twelve to thirty acres, were measured off to each family—partly clear land, and partly wooded. Leases of these farms were granted them for seven years, at the rate of one pound per acre of yearly rental for the clear land—the wooded land being rent free for four years."

This settlement of the *Midlothian* Highlanders on Dunmore was known colloquially as "Skye." The Highlanders were careful and clever with their limited resources, constructing their houses out of saplings with reed or bark roofs; making their initial government ration of two months' beef last four months; and in some cases, making porridge and bread from Indian corn and maize meal. Like all work in agriculture, their first four years were typical—1838 a good year; 1839 drought; 1840 flood; and 1841 good grain crop but abysmally low prices. While there was no record of trouble with the Indigenous inhabitants, the group was attacked by bushrangers who were able to get away with a quantity of money.

The twins, Malcolm and Donald, were the ones in the family to carry the name of Gillies into the future. Now turning seventeen, they set out to ensure they knew all they could about farming even to have their own houses before finding wives and raising families. They worked as farm labourers, contractors, tenant farmers with their father, builders, shearers, dairymen, and riverboat hands.

The following story has been extracted from the *Maitland Mercury* of February, March, and April 1846 which recounts the "Hillsborough murder." At the time, Donald and Malcolm were working at a property at Hillsborough about ten kilometres north of Maitland. On the same property, an Irishman, William Shea, and a Scotsman, Andrew Menzies, were partners but dirt poor. Menzies disappeared, but with the help of the Indigenous trackers who were attracted by ants, some carrying maggots, between the two men's houses, immediately traced them to where Menzies's body lay. The Gillies men gave evidence to the court of conversations they had with both men. These convinced the court that Shea was lying about his innocence. He was found guilty and hung a couple of weeks later.

In 1854, two events took place that caused a sharp turn in the futures of Malcolm and Donald. The first was the death of their father, Don, at sixty-five years of age. The second event that presaged Malcolm's move into the world of capitalism appeared in the *Maitland Mercury* and the *Hunter River General Advertiser* on Saturday, May 13, 1854.

Malcolm Gillies:The Early Capitalist

That Advertisement

And as so often happens, future large situations culminate from an initial decision made about a small event.

Unprecedented Sale of 2000 Acres of Rich Agriculture Land
With Five Miles Frontage to the Hunter River
To be subdivided into Farms

Mr. A. Dodds has received instructions from
the trustees of the late V Jacob, Esq.,
to announce to the public that the Valuable
Estate of MILLER'S FOREST
containing 2000 Acres will be submitted to public
competition in the month of May.

The Estate has been surveyed into farms of about 50 Acres each
Title a Grant from the Crown
Full description of the farms will be given in a future advertisement

[On Saturday, May 20, the advertisement ran that "the public competition would be held on Monday, May 29, 1854, at 12 o'clock.]

It is interesting that what are called auctions today were called "public competitions" in 1854.

Malcolm and Donald, both now thirty-three years old and unmarried, were each able to buy a farm of twenty acres, and now was the time to be married and raise a family. Malcolm espied, courted, and married Margaret McPherson in the bride's father's house, 56 Gloucester Street, The Rocks, Sydney, on November 5, 1856. Margaret's parents were Alexander and Isabella McPherson; there was also a younger brother, Ewen, aged five. They arrived in South Australia on the *Tomatin* in 1840.

The biography from here follows the line of Judy's great-grandfather, Malcolm. In farewells to twin Donald, it is noted that a year later, he took Miss Jane Martin for his bride.

So what is the stuff that made Don and the others larger-than-life farmers? Even today it is a long way from Scotland to Australia!

Not much can be said about the daily grind of farm life. Indeed, living on the land does not seem to have changed from the 1850s to the 2010s. Work daylight to dark, droughts, floods, crop failures, good seasons, bad seasons, low prices, sickness, childbirth, death, schooling, limited employment, the banks. Malcolm had arrived in the area of Miller's Forest in 1837 and had worked for others for seventeen years. He obtained his own property in 1854, and twenty-five years later, in 1879, had been battling the elements for over forty years. He was fifty-six years old and could only wonder about the future for him, Margaret, and his family.

Major decisions are never made easily, but the decision to sell up and move to Sydney was presaged in the *Maitland Mercury* and *Hunter River General Advertiser* Saturday, November 8, 1879. It is noteworthy that the types of purchasers he was seeking were firstly capitalists and secondly speculators. The word "capitalist" was first used in 1774 in an essay by Turgot, "Reflections on the Formation and Distribution of Wealth," to describe individuals of a certain social class. A capitalist is best defined as a person who has capital invested in business. A speculator is a capitalist who, by using what might be described as dubious investment strategies, attempts in a shorter timeframe to outperform traditional longer-term investors.

FIRST-CLASS INVESTMENT
To Capitalists, Speculators, Farmers and Others
20 ACRES
MAGNIFICENT ALLUVIAL LAND
THE PICK OF
MILLER'S FOREST
WITH
DEEP WATER FRONTAGE
TO THE
HUNTER RIVER

SPARKE & CLIFT have received instructions from
Mr. Malcolm Gillies, to sell by auction, at
Brown's (late Fullford's) Hotel, West Maitland, on
FRIDAY, 21st November, 1879, at Two o'clock

20 ACRES MAGNIFICENT ALLUVIAL LAND
With Deep Water Frontage to Hunter River
situated at Miller's Forest, and without doubt

the pick Farm of the whole of the Miller's
Forest Estate. The Land is at present cropped
with Lucerne and Millet, and is famed for its prolific crops.

The decision came back to the family that the farm had run out of room. Their answer was that, as much as possible, to continue to keep together as they had been in Scotland, their trip on the *Midlothian*, and the years at Miller's Forest. For the younger ones, going to Sydney would provide superior schooling. For the young men, employment was available, and an adequate health system existed.

Real estate advertising in the *Maitland Mercury* and *Hunter River General Advertiser* on Saturday, November 22, 1879, provides information about the £831 Malcolm could bring with him to Sydney as, it would be said these days, his pension:

Land Sale by Messrs. Sparke & Clift.

As announced by advertisement in our columns,
Messrs. Sparke & Clift held a sale of land yesterday,
at Brown's (late Fullford's) Hotel, West Maitland.
The attendance of intending purchasers was large,
And the lot submitted to competition found purchasers at a very satisfactory figure as follows:-

On account of Mr. Malcolm Gillies:
20 Acre Farm at Miller's Forest, with improvements
thereon, to Mr. Greaves for £801. The growing
crop was taken at a valuation, £30 being the
price fixed. The purchaser paid cash for the whole.

It is hard to assess what this amount of money means in today's money value, but the lowest face-value lift based on simple annual inflation would have £A 831 (1879) = AUD 130,000 (2017). It is hard to believe that a purchaser was carrying around £831 cash in his back pocket. They surely must have gone round to one of the banks in the larger towns such as Maitland to hand over the money.

Malcolm and Margaret's family grew in number. Some were given a second name, some not. The list is as follows. Note the question marks next to the female children.

	Born	Died	
Malcolm	1821	1909	
Margaret	1833	1921	
Alexander McPherson	1858	1923	
Donald	1860	1884	
James Hyndes	1861	1942	
James McCulloch	1865	1932	
William McPherson	1865	1941	
John	1867	1950	
Lawrence	1869	1870	(died of whooping cough aged seven months)
Malcolm	1871	1894	(died in Redfern railway accident Nov. 2, 1894)
Catherine Isabella	?	?	
Anne	1880?	?	

It is assumed that the family moved to the suburb of Petersham in Sydney. Following are snippets of the lives of various family members:

- Malcolm, the head of his small clan lived and died at Tenelba, 159 New Canterbury Road, Petersham, at eighty-nine years from senile decay. According to death certificates, he, Margaret, and Annie were of the Brethren persuasion.
- Margaret had arrived in Sydney at seven years of age in 1840 and had a full life of eighty-eight years. She was married only to Malcolm and had eleven children. One son died in babyhood. Three other sons died at ages eighteen, twenty, and twenty-four. The youngest daughter did not marry, whilst the six others survived to marry and raise families, though not as large as hers.
- Alexander McPherson, their first child, was named, as usual, after his wife's father, and the family name was the name of the clan to which the Gillieses belonged. He stayed in the Newcastle area, where he found employment.
- Donald only lived only to age twenty-four, but the cause of his early demise has not been found.

- James Hyndes, called Jim, has been best described in his younger days as "a sanguine, enthusiastic little man with bright eyes." He was a dreamer, inventor, and industrialist. His first wish was to study for the Presbyterian ministry, but following his 1886 marriage to Annie Griffiths, he sold real estate for the next eight years through the Eastern Suburbs Agency Co. at Paddington. In 1905, he became manager of the Gillies Sulphide Concentrating Machine Ltd. There were patents to treat tailings from the Block 10 Mine at Broken Hill. The attempt failed. His schemes were numerous. He died "disillusioned … frail… disappointed."
- James McCulloch, his second name coming from the name of the clergyman who baptised him, was always known as Cull. He and his wife, Jesse, had four children—Elsie (1890?), Ewen (1891?), McCulloch (1893?), and Allan (1894). They lived in Sydney, where Cull was an estate agent with his elder brother.
- William McPherson went to live in Western Australia. He was a grocer by trade also known for his painting ability. He was married to Amanda James in 1891, and their seven children were Cyril Stanley, Winifred (twin deceased), Norman, Alfred, William Keith, and Gertrude. Cyril was also known for his painting ability.
- John, Judy's grandfather, would have undertaken some level of apprenticeship in clothing after which he set up his own business as a tailor and men's haberdasher in Orange, NSW.
- Lawrence was born in 1869 and died of whooping cough at the age of seven months.
- Malcolm was born in 1871, and in 1892, he married Emily Smith. Tragically, on November 2, 1894, he died as the result of severe scalds on the face, throat, and arms, and shock when he was near a train engine that exploded at Redfern station.
- Catherine Isabella is only known to be named after her aunt and her maternal grandmother. Her married name was Lane.

References are made to eleven children, but apart from a passing mention of Catherine Isabella and Anne, it almost seems that girls didn't count!

John Gillies: "Business Entrepreneur"

The biographical line highlights John Gillies (Judy's grandfather) who was waiting "to find" Lily Anderson Beveridge so the ancestral line would continue to Judy.

As Far Away from Farming as Possible

Judy's grandfather, John Gillies, was born on May 26, 1867, at the family home in Miller's Forest, Raymond Terrace NSW. John's father, Malcolm, had "made his pile," as told earlier, and between late-1879 to 1880, he moved his family to Sydney. This decision was simply be for the wellbeing of the family in education, health, and employment.

The author's preferred facetious opinion is that nobody wants to live in the area of Hexham and the abutting Millers Forest with their local Hexham Grey mosquito species (*Ochlerotatus alternans).* (The Australian colloquialism for mosquitoes is "mozzies.") These Hexham Grey mosquitoes were enormous, ferocious, and are part of the folklore of Australia. As one of Australia's present bush poets, Bob Skelton, so well put it,

The Territory has large crocodiles
Queensland the Taipan snake
And wild scrub bulls are the biggest risk over in the Western State
But if you're in the premier State, round Hunter Valley way
Look out for them giant mozzies, the dreaded Hexham Grey.

And so, in 1881, John was in Sydney learning the skills to become a clothier. He joined Walter Lance and Co., Clothier and Drapers, of Sydney, which was an interesting company in its own right. Walter Lance, at the age of nineteen, had set himself up in business as a general draper at Bull St, Birmingham, England. He immigrated to Sydney, bringing sixty-five cases of merchandise with him, and immediately commenced business. Walter expanded his interests, opening a clothing store in Wollongong on October 19, 1889; Lance's son Frederick, at nineteen, was one of the managers. John was working at this store, and two years later, when Walter Lance opened another store in Orange, John was fortuitously put in charge, the company being not averse to using young people in senior roles. This move to Orange indicates that John was not a stale-stodgy-stay-at-home man but someone who could follow his profession for fame and fortune.

It was two years later that John bought the Walter Lance business in Orange and set himself up as "J. Gillies—Clothier, Tailor, Mercer and Outfitter." With the security base of a business, four years later, October 13, 1896, he married Lily Anderson Beveridge.

John Gillies's first shop in Summer Street, Orange.

The shop was located next to, and on the ground floor under the Empire Hotel with a strategic location on the corners of Summer and Peisly Streets. He threw himself into advertising in the local *Leader* newspaper and, for example, in the Saturday, February 1906, edition it read:

*** A RICH FIND OF GOLD is of interest to everyone.
How to save money should be of equal interest.
You'll save it by going to J Gillies' clothing, mercery and hat sale
Next Empire Hotel, Summer Street***

John comes across as an entrepreneur prepared to purchase a business and then prepared to expand. His foray into a second shop was in Cadia, where gold and copper were discovered in 1851. This small mining village is on the southern edge of Mount Conobolas. The village is reached travelling the twenty-one kilometres around the eastern edge of the mount. This mine continues today and is now owned by Newcrest Mining and known as Cadia Valley Operations. It is one of Australia's largest gold and copper mining operations.

Chilcott Street, Cadia Village, NSW (1904).

John's outpost at Cadia was more a general store than a clothier. It is halfway down Chilcott Street on the right-hand side, with two children standing in front of the darkened portico. In 1921, a fire engulfed the buildings along that side, including John's General Store. He never returned to Cadia.

John's son Mal (Judy's dad) had worked in the shop during the mid-1930s but after the war, there was no return to the shop as Grandfather John had sold the business. This has been attributed to the onset of blindness. Judy remembers her visit to him with her brother, John, around 1947, during which time their grandfather would pass his hands over their faces and hands to envisage their appearances.

Grandfather John Gillies.

He died in Orange in 1950 at the age of eighty-three.

Judy's Father's Antecedents: Grandmother's Line

Lily Anderson Gillies (nee Beveridge): "The Orphan"

Judy's grandmother, Lily Anderson Beveridge, was born in St George Parish, Edinburgh, Scotland, on April 10, 1874. She had an unsettled childhood that started when she was two years old with the death of her mother, Janet Beveridge (nee Bonnar) on January 1, 1876, at the age of twenty-six. The bereaved father, Laurence Beveridge, then married Annie Hood Bruce. The year 1880 was an eventful time for the six-year-old Lily. In addition to the new stepmother, she was uprooted from Scotland to immigrate to Australia. The family group consisted of Lily, her father, stepmother, stepsister Elizabeth Bruce Beveridge, plus Laurence's elder sister Lilias and her husband, Robert Anderson. The small family reached South Australia from Glasgow on the *Loch Garry* on September 26, 1880.

Documentation indicates that Laurence was a member of the Brethren Sect. His occupation was as a sculptor, and two drinking fountains located in Hyde Park near St Mary's Cathedral were carved by him from Pyrmont stone. These fountains were gifted by a Mr John Frazer in the 1880s to the people of Sydney, a time when many houses lacked water connections. Laurence had produced a similar Gothic memorial in Tain, Scotland. This artistic trait has not seemed to appear in his descendants.

On October 12, 1883, after only three years in the colony, Laurence died from typhoid fever at thirty-five years of age, in his home, 3 Alva Terrace, Camden Street, Newtown. He had worked from 237 Elizabeth Street, Sydney. The nine-year-old orphan, Lily, was taken into the care of her father's elder sister, Lilias, and her husband, Robert Anderson. One notes that her stepmother did not pick up the responsibility of raising Lily. Two apparent reasons for this decision were that her stepmother, Annie, was now a widow with two children of her own to nurture, and secondly, Lilias was married to a man who was a railway stationmaster, and thus had a steady income. And Lilias was barren in a culture in which children were expected. Through Lily, she could release her maternal instincts.

To appreciate what found Lily in the Orange district, it is appropriate to review the 1879 rail-bridge collapse into the Tay River.

The Great Tay River Rail-Bridge Disaster

In 1890, a Mr William McGonagall made his poetic reputation with the following work; two verses are shown:

The Tay Bridge Disaster

Beautiful Railway Bridge of the Silv'ry Tay!
Alas! I am very sorry to say
That ninety lives have been taken away
On the last Sabbath day of 1879
Which will be remembered for a very long time

Twas about seven o'clock at night
And the wind it blew with all its might,—
And the Demon of the air seem'd to say
I'll blow down the Bridge of Tay

For twenty years, Robert Anderson had worked predominantly in the historic county of Fife, situated between the Firth of Tay to the north and the Firth of Forth to the south. To go north from Edinburgh was to ferry across the Firth of Forth, train across Fife, ferry across the Firth of Tay to Dundee, and then train northward as desired.

For the thousands of years of "the good old days," the speed of travel was never faster than that of the horse. As the Iron Horse began to take over, speed caught the imagination of the travelling public, and they soon demanded that rail bridges should cross the Firth of Tay and the Firth of Forth. It would all make the London to Aberdeen trip five hours shorter. The first river to be crossed was the Tay.

Mr Thomas Bouch was the designer and overseer of the building of the bridge, which opened on June 1, 1878. It looked impressive, being almost two miles across the firth and with girders twenty-seven metres above the water to allow ships from Perth to pass underneath. A year later, June 20, 1879, Queen Victoria crossed the bridge travelling back from Balmoral to Windsor and saved an hour of time. She knighted Bouch three weeks later. It was the pinnacle of his career, and he basked in his glory as he anticipated more accolades with his appointment to be the designer and builder of the bridge to traverse the Firth of Forth.

However, a strategic fault had slipped through the design process with no allowance for wind loading being incorporated into the engineer's drawings. The old cliché, "It was a dark and stormy night," might convey some sense of impending doom and the night of Sunday, December 27, 1879, it was truly dark with a raging storm carrying winds of 10 to 11 on the Beaufort scale (89 to 117 km/hour). The winds were also blowing at right angles to the train, which would provide the most destructive forces. One witness watching the northbound train leave for Dundee told how he saw sparks from the wheels on the east side. This had continued for no more than three minutes. By then, the train was in the high girders, and there was a sudden bright flash of light. All disappearing at the same instant, falling into the depths of the Tay River, killing all on board, some seventy-five to one hundred souls. An exact number of those travelling that night was never established. The next morning, a fruitless search for survivors was underway.

The search for survivors. Note high girders at the top left of the drawing.

Following the catastrophe, Sir Thomas Bouch's life spiralled downwards. His design for the Forth Bridge had been accepted and the foundation stone laid, but the project was taken from him. The public enquiry concluded that the Tay Bridge had been "badly designed, badly built and badly maintained." With all the shock and distress, Sir Thomas's health rapidly gave way, and he died ten months after the collapse, on October 30, 1880.

Robert Anderson and the Tay Bridge disaster were part of the family history and regularly discussed from the memories of Grandfather John and Aunt Lilias. It was said that Robert was employed at the Dundee end of the bridge, but whilst not being directly involved in the actual disaster, he was affected by it. Today, the diagnosis would be post-traumatic stress disorder (PTSD). Six months after the disaster, he and Lilias had packed their bags and were on their way to Australia with the Beveridges. He was well respected in the railway community and was presented with a French clock with the inscription,

Presented to Mr Robert Anderson
As a mark of esteem
On his leaving for Australia
After 20 years' service as Station Agent
North British (NB) Railway
Faulkland Road Fife
June 1880

Judy's cousin Don still has that clock bedecking his lounge room.

Robert returned to the railways following his arrival in Sydney. He was duly appointed the first stationmaster in the village of Borenore, about eighteen kilometres west of Orange on the Broken Hill line. This predated December 21, 1885, when the first train arrived at the new station. The "wheels" that got Lily to the Orange district started with a nine-year-old orphan and a rail disaster that shook Scotland to its core. But here she was, in Orange, an indomitable figure at twenty-two years old, where she had

Grandmother Lily Beveridge.

met and married John Gillies. There is also another sense of the wheels of progress, in this case at its worst. The Borenore station is now closed and is being used by the local tennis club.

A Busy Mother

The new family settled down to family life, and within the year, the first of their six children was born. They were: Lilian Janet (September 29, 1897), Winifred Margaret (1899), Laurence Beveridge (1900), Miriam Elizabeth (unknown), Malcolm McPherson (1907), and John Frederick (1909), who was always known as Uncle Fred rather than Uncle John.

By 1921, with the eldest of the children at twenty-four and the youngest at twelve, the May 2 advertisement in the *Leader* caught Lily's eye:

> AN ATTRACTIVE PROJECT
> An opportunity that many have been waiting for, will be available to them on Thursday May 15th, when Messrs J Nancarrow and Co will offer by auction the property known as The Australian Arms Hotel. The building is substantially constructed of brick, contains thirteen rooms with outbuildings of four-stall stable sheds etc. ... We may suppose there will be hot competition for such first-class situation for residential purposes.

The old Australian Arms Hotel, Orange.

The sale's report from *The Leader* of May 13 said it all:

PROPERTY SALES

Messrs J Nancarrow and Co report having sold by auction yesterday that land-mark of early Orange, the old Australian Arms Hotel, for the executors of the late Mrs. H McFadden. There was a good attendance of buyers, and bidding was brisk, the property being knocked down to Mrs J Gillies at £700.

This suggested purchase by Grandmother Lily has provided animated discussion amongst the family. The issue is whether grandmother, a member of the Plymouth Brethren, would purchase a house that once was a hotel, even though it had been delicensed for ten years.

In the Electoral Roll of 1921, the Gillies were living at 109 March Street, whilst by the 1925 roll, they were established in 53 Sale Street. Lily was known as a pianist, and a grand piano graced the home. Husband John, with his Plymouth Brethren background, was not amused, but she would quietly wait for him to leave the house, and in modern parlance, the homestead would then rock. She also provided her talents to the local church.

Lily had seen her six children grow to adulthood, some with children of their own. In the following photo, the family, from left to right, was Grandfather John, Grandmother Lily, Lillian, Laurence, John Frederick, Miriam, Malcolm, and Winifred. The best understanding of the children is from Lillian (Gartrill) as being Reginald, Neville, Leslie, and Brenda.

The Gillies clan, Orange (c. 1930).
Mal, back row, far right.

The newspaper notification of Lily's son Mal, Judy's father's passing read as follows:

GILLIES: *Malcolm McPherson, -*
November 15, 1976, at hospital late of Manly,
Dearly loved husband of Freda, loved father and father-in-law
of Judith and Robert, John and Fay and fond grandfather of their children.

CHAPTER 6

My 'Ain Folk

One can never be too careful in the choice of one's parents ... and their parents ... and their parents ... again-and-again, for that is how one's own set of genes developed.

—Sighted in quora.com

If you know your ancestry, then you know who to blame.

—"Feeling Short? Blame Your Ancestors," ABC Science

A List of Characters

The previous chapter highlighted Judy's two ancestral bloodlines on her father's side. Looking at Judy's female line, the grandfather was

Frederick Lamont McFadzean, who was among the list of characters (see "There's Gold in Them Thar Hills").

From Judy's grandmother's female line (grandmother had been born Alice Edith Akhurst) that bloodline's characters had included Johann Ludwig Kitz, "The Germanic Link." And further back, William Mower and Ellen Akhurst, with William being labelled "A Bohemian Down Under."

The book has lingered with William Mower Akhurst and his wife, Ellen. Why? Because either he and/or Ellen were the actual start of a specific showtime gene pool. It appeared during their own theatrical activities and flowed on to their descendants who have shown a musical streak and wild artistic temperament. One of their children was Sidney Philip Akhurst, of whom there is no knowledge of his personality. He did, however, marry Germanic Alice Kitz, and whilst anything can be read into a photo, an imperious gaze looks out scrutinizing the world to determine who he can control next.

Alice Akhurst (nee Kitz).

Sidney and Alice had six children; five reached adulthood. Their first child was Alice Edith Akhurst (1881–1954), Judy's grandmother, whom she remembers well. There were three other sisters—Ethel Rose, Beatrice Ellen, and Mildred Freda—who were known throughout Orange for their exuberance.

Alice was assertive and had her Freda reciting to an audience by three years of age. There were more than adequate external factors to spark her show business trait. As mentioned previously, when Freda was ten, the *Orange Leader* newspaper reported on June 18, 1919,

> Miss Iris Flower's Recital
> For her recital of "Dadsy and Babsy" with pianoforte accompaniment by Miss Gladys Mackenzie, little Miss Freda McFadzean received tumultuous applause and was also rewarded with a floral tribute.

Judy's Mother's Antecedents: Grandfather's Line

Frederick Lamont McFadzean, "There's Gold in Them Thar Hills"

Judy's grandfather, Frederick Lamont McFadzean, was born on March 14, 1873, at Sandhurst, Bendigo, Victoria. His parents were Mathew and Isabella McFadzean. In the recording of Frederick's birth, Mathew, as the father, recorded his profession as a "mining speculator," a prescience of what his son would be in his later years.

Frederick's life split into two parts. The first was his time living in Prahran, Melbourne. He was known for his political activism in the Prahran Branch of the Australian Natives Association (ANA). The ANA was a mutual fund founded in Melbourne in April 1871, whose members were restricted to white men born in Australia. Outside its mutual charter, it provided drive for matters such as federation and later, "The White Australia Policy." There was also the world of debating in the Prahran Presbyterian Literary and Debating Society.

The second part occurred around 1910, when Frederick and Alice moved to and set up home in Orange, NSW. This was to get away from the asthma he was suffering in Melbourne. He was involved as a commercial traveller for Robert Harper and Company throughout western NSW, a director of three gold-mining companies, and a well-known flower expert both in displaying and judging.

The Prahran Days

Frederick Lamont McFadzean, Judy's grandfather.

Frederick was born in Bendigo, Victoria. The last references to him in the press were firstly, his election to the Metropolitan Committee of the Prahran Branch of the ANA on November 30, 1907, and secondly, his marriage on April 8, 1908. He had been living in the house named Merriwa in Prahran, a suburb of Melbourne, and from there, he was married to Alice Edith Akhurst of Excalibur of St Kilda at the Holy Trinity Church, Brighton Road, Balaclava, Melbourne. The bride entered the church to a Highland wedding march played by a Scottish piper. After the service, a reception and wedding tea was held at the St Kilda Town Hall. The couple honeymooned at Warburton, Victoria.

Political Activism

As mentioned previously, Frederick was a member of the ANA. His name first reached the press (*Prahran Chronicle*, November 26, 1898) when at twenty-five years old, he was elected to the Committee of the Prahran Branch and to be the press correspondent at the upcoming conference. He went on to be vice president in early 1904, and then was unopposed for the presidency on December 3, 1905.

In his early administrative work, Frederick was one of the organisers of a political meeting on December 8, 1900, that agreed that "a Branch of the National Liberal Organisation be formed in Prahran." The gathering was informed that the Honourable Alfred Deakin would be present at a future meeting. Deakin, in due course, became the second prime minister of Australia.

Prahran Literary and Debating Society

Frederick was strong in honing his speaking skills and was, for example, part of the discussion on the contention that Beatrice Harridan's novel, *The Fowler*, contained swearing such as "damn." Some said yes, others indicated that it was slang. The *Prahran Chronicle* (June 30, 1900) did not indicate which side of the issue Frederick took.

The inaugural meeting of the society was held on February 17, 1900, and Frederick was elected to both the committee and to be the press correspondent. References in the *Prahran Chronicle* have him involved in the following debates:

1898-Aug-13: "Female Suffrage"
1899-Mar-04: "Is State Socialism desirable?"
1901-Aug-17: "That it is desirable that we have the Referendum"
1902-Jul-05: "Should the Victorian Government accept the Kyabram Program?"

The Days at Orange

There are no records as to when Frederick and Alice left Melbourne, but the driving force was Frederick's bad asthma. It is not known why, amongst the many country towns, Orange was chosen, but chosen it was. Considering events that occurred around that period, 1908 would appear the most probable time. The most intriguing event that led to that suggested date was the birth of their first daughter, and Judy's mother, Freda, on January 12, 1909, at Studleigh, Haberfield, a suburb of Sydney. There was no birth notice in a Sydney paper, but one appeared in the Melbourne *Argus* with the obvious intention that all their Victorian friends would be kept informed with the now "out-of-staters." The other deduction from this Sydney birth was that Frederick and Alice, having already moved to Orange, would use the nearest big-city doctor for the first birth.

The latest date for the shift would have to be a time significantly before June 4, 1912, when following the tennis match between Orange and Dubbo, "Mr. F.L. McFadzean proposed a toast to the Dubbo team" (*The Leader*, June 4, 1912). The reasoning for this timing is that Frederick had to have adequate time to become known for both his tennis and speaking skills.

Hine Taimoa, 66 Kite Street (and 12 Hill Street), Orange

The McFadzeans arrived in Orange and bought Hine Taimoa. This block had a long depth from the street, which allowed for a large entertaining room called The Court at the rear of the house. Parties followed parties. Typically, "One of the jolliest parties of the week was given by Freda McFadzean at Orange in honour of her cousin Miss Iris Parks from Melbourne and the guests numbered about 50 … The large room and hall were gay with jazz streamers, coloured balloons and Japanese lanterns, casting a soft glow on the youthful throng" (*The Sun* [Sydney], December 19, 1926).

Out the back was a vegetable garden containing a large fig tree and a full-size, clay tennis court with plum trees running down both sides of the court. This was a very "in" place to be invited for tennis. Over the years, some of the afternoons had been graced by Daphne Akhurst, Jack Crawford, and Harry Hopman. Daphne was Judy's mother's cousin and an Australian tennis star of the late 1920s. Her country's respect of her prowess was evidenced in the choice to use her name on the perpetual cup presented to the winner of the ladies singles Australian championship. Jack Crawford was the world's number one tennis player in 1933, and Harry Hopman was the runner-up in the 1930, 1931, and 1932 Australian men's singles championships. Harry was respected as the architect of Australia's postwar tennis supremacy in the Davis Cup.

As old age crept up, the glory days of Kite Street faded, and sometime after 1946, the McFadzeans downsized to 12 Hill Street, further away from the town centre, to a modest, two or three bed bungalow, with just a single garage down the back. Judy's brother, John, remembers visiting it when he was around eight or nine years old.

Robert Harper and Company

Frederick's representation was highly respected in the community, and after more than ten years of service, mention was made in the "Social" section in the *Dubbo Dispatch* and *Wellington Independent* newspapers (June 9, 1922): "Mr. F. L. McFadzean has, for many years, been the trusted and enterprising representative for Robert Harper & Co. and is now enjoying 3 months leave."

Director of Gold-Mining Companies

From observation, one can see that the "gold bug" can be as dangerous as any bacterium, and Frederick certainly caught the disease. Beginning around 1921, he left the steady employment of Harper's to become, as his father, a mining speculator. He was soon bobbing up and down across the goldfields around Orange being manager, managing director or shareholder in the following companies:

Lucknow Gold Mines No Liability (NL)
Lucknow 66 Gold-Mining Company NL
Lucknow Pups Gold Mining Company NL
Lucknow Reward Gold Mining Syndicate
Lucknow Sulphides NL
Manna Hill Gold Mining Company NL
North Hawkins Hill NL
North Bismarck (Lucknow) Gold Mines NL
Shaw River Alluvials NL
South Lucknow Gold Mining Company NL
South Lucknow Extended Gold Mining Company NL

The modus operandi that appeared to be played out was that once a mine looked as if its future productive life was limited, it would be liquidated and another company set up to replace it. The two South

Lucknow companies went into liquidation on January 20, 1939. Perhaps this is a tad coincidental, but it was in September of that year that Frederick's granddaughter, Judy, the woman of gold, was born in Orange.

Advertising, it is said, never goes astray, and who is out there to spread the word but our very own, F. L. McFadzean, the well-known "super-optimist" of the group:

> Lucknow Pups.
>
> Advice from Orange makes it appear as though Lucknow Pups has developed into a good position for a strike of rich ore. If this eventuates some of the hats in Orange will be several days in coming down again. Presumably a "plane will have to be despatched to recover that of F.L. McFadzean, the super-optimist of the group. All recent gold mines have found everything but the gold and 'twould be a pleasant change if the Pups got it by the hatful. ("Labour Day" paper of September 1925)
>
> Manna Hill Gold.
>
> Mr. McFadzean, who is interested in mining generally in the west, and who has an interest in the Manna Hill Gold Mining Co. was in town yesterday. He had with him gold "won" from the Manna Hill mine worth £300. The gold created quite a lot of interest amongst the people of this town, and the hope was expressed that similar strikes might be made in this district." (*Wellington Times,* March 5, 1931)

Floral Expert

The *Western Champion* paper of May 6, 1920 read, "Mr F. McFadzean, the well-known floral expert, has been specially engaged by the committee to judge next Wednesday (12th) and Thursday (13th), the floral exhibits at the Autumn Flower Show run in conjunction with the Presbyterian Church."

Frederick sometimes exhibited his own range, including at the Gilgandra show of November 1918, yellow roses, six-bloom snapdragons, six-bloom anemones, ranunculi, and foxgloves. His signature flower was the Sulphur Queen Dahlia. In the meantime, Alice, his wife, received first prize for the best decorated table.

Last Days

The McFadzeans continued to live at 12 Hill Street, Orange, until Alice died in 1952. Frederick then came to Seaforth, a Sydney suburb near Manly, to live in Judy's family's Plant Street home from 1952 to 1953. His was a small room in the semi-basement. With the family calling him "Pop," he used to claim "he was Popeye the sailor man."

For the eternal optimist, his last days were sad. There never was any mother lode of gold. When his dear Alice had preceded him, he had had to leave Orange. Freda eventually could not cope, and for his last two years, he lived out his life in a nursing home in Mosman. His gold optimism would break out to the end, and he would stress to Mal, his son-in-law, that the shares he and Mal held would, one day, "come good!" Some of the gold companies' scrip still exists in Judy's brother's archival cache.

Frederick Lamont McFadzean died March 24, 1958, at Mosman, Sydney.

Judy's Mother's Antecedents: Grandmother's Line

Alice Edith McFadzean (nee Akhurst)

To refresh your memory, Judy's grandmother, Alice Edith Akhurst, was born in 1881 at Carlton, a northern suburb close to the city centre of Melbourne. She married Frederick Lamont McFadzean April 8, 1908, in Melbourne and shortly moved to Orange NSW, where their three daughters—Freda Sidney, Hazel Lamont, and Nancy Alice—blossomed.

For Alice, the keywords of life were "parties" and "hospitality." She required help as the following advertisement in *The Leader* of Friday, July 11, 1919, indicates: "Wanted—General, all duties no washing Apply Mrs McFadzean, 'Hine Tamoa' Kite Street."

A Miss Gwen Jones was chosen and got along well with the three daughters. In time, Alice and Frederick adopted Gwen into the family.

One of the Orange Hospital's fund-raising activities was the publishing of a cookery book compiled of Orange ladies' favourite recipes. It is not known whether the one provided by Alice was her signature recipe, her *piece de resistance,* but it was a quite simple recipe:

Arrowroot Cake

> Three eggs and 3/4 cup sugar beaten to a cream, 3/4 cup arrowroot, 2 small teaspoons baking powder, pinch of salt. Cook for twenty minutes.
>
> —Mrs. F. L. McFadzean, Hine Taimoa, Kite Street, Orange

She died on May 29, 1952, at Orange, NSW.

William Mower Akhurst: "A Bohemian Down Under"

"Once upon a time, well actually on Wednesday, June 20, 1849, the good barque *Posthumous* of 390 ton berthed at Port Adelaide in the colony of South Australia." This was the same type of vessel on which Captain Cook sailed to reach Australia in 1770. Both for James Cook and for those on the *Posthumous,* there were no reporters to greet them.

Adelaide then had a population of 11,000, whilst the Colony of South Australia had 52,904, 13,824 of whom had settled there in the same year as the Akhursts. In 1850, the colony was described as "a country very much resembling the South of Europe, but where Englishmen are governed by laws to which they have been accustomed, and where the habits of social life are such as British subjects understand and appreciate … and that even though the Colony is very young, the comforts and refinements of civilised life are understood and can be enjoyed."

But why our interest in this barque's arrival? It was simply that amongst the intrepid sailors was the family of William Mower Akhurst, his wife, Ellen, and their son, Adrian. William and Ellen were Judy's great-great-grandparents and the first of the family on her mother's side who came to Australia. There was also the quaintness of "Mower" as a second name.

Mower was also imagined as the initiator of the show business gene line. In later family conversations, this was changed to Ellen as the musical trendsetter, the Sullivan of Gilbert and Sullivan. Unsurprisingly for us, they ended up with the name of the Punch and Judy Show.'

Both Mower and Ellen brought with them an ambition for success in the arts in the colonies. William first found work as a dramatic author and journalist. For the fifteen years they first lived in Australia, William would establish a reputation—especially in Melbourne—as a writer and adapter of pantomimes and comic sketches for the theatre.

Some Early History of William Mower Akhurst

In his national obituary, Mower was remembered as a "big, jolly man" and as "a thorough Bohemian ... and a most congenial companion." Not a word in common use today, a Bohemian defined one who lived an artistic lifestyle, placing freedom of self-expression above all other desires, including wealth, social conformity, and status.

Source: National Library of Australia

Mower was born in London on December 29, 1822, the first of five children born to William Akhurst and his wife, Harriet Dickinson. William Akhurst was a linen-draper living in Brook Street, in the

Hammersmith district of London, and where they would live most of their lives. In 1837, "the inhabitants of Hammersmith were amongst the most forward in their demonstrations of loyalty upon the auspicious occasion of Her Majesty Queen Victoria's first journey to Windsor after her happy accession to the throne." On the Broadway, where William Akhurst was recorded as living in the 1841 census, "a splendid triumphal arch was erected ... tastefully decorated with a profusion of laurel and other evergreens, interspersed with flowers, and the summit surmounted with a crown, composed of the choicest flowers then in season." It is easy to imagine the involvement of William and Harriet Akhurst with their son William Mower and their other children enjoying these events that came with residing in a town that was quickly growing into a district of Greater London thanks to the industrial revolution on the cusp of the Victorian Age.

The Akhurst family, as far as is known, hailed originally from the small village of Sheldwich and the hamlet of Leaveland, located in the county of Kent in the south east corner of England. Mower's father, William Akhurst, was christened on November 21, 1793, in Sheldwich, Kent. His parents and William Mower Akhurst's grandparents were James Akhurst (b. 1765) and Mary Rye (b. 1762), who were married on October 1, 1791. This James Akhurst was the son of wheelwright James Akhurst (b. 1743 in Leaveland, Kent) and his wife, Mary Parker. James and Mary were married on January 26, 1765, in Leaveland, Kent, and their only known child was James. There is nothing in William Mower's family's previous antecedent line that suggested there were genes that would take him onto the stage, the Gilbert of Gilbert and Sullivan.

Some Early History of Ellen Akhurst (nee Tully)

Ellen and her twin brother, George Tully, were born in London on February 14, 1824. She and William Mower Akhurst were married on October 26, 1845, in St George's Church, Bloomsbury in London, where they spent their early married life. At that time, Mower was working as a merchant (possibly with his father), and Ellen was an actress. Ellen came from a family involved in the arts. Her father, Thomas Howard Tully, was a musician. Her mother was Sophia, nee Shingley.

Her older brother, James Howard Tully (1814–1868), was also musician as well as a composer who was "active in the Lyceum and Covent Garden Opera Houses." The obituary for James Howard Tully appeared in *The Australasian* in 1868 due to his high standing in the musical circles of London and his connection to Australia as Ellen Akhurst's brother. It read as follows, transcribed from the *Daily Telegraph*:

> We regret to announce the death of this popular composer, so well known to the general public as the orchestral conductor at the Theatre Royal, Drury-lane. Mr. J.H Tully, who only a few days indisposed, died yesterday afternoon from the effects of a severe attack of bronchitis. His decease will be deeply deployed by a large number of professional friends, who held him in the highest esteem; and in the theatre, which has for many years profited by his zeal, skill, and musical experience, his place will not easily be supplied. Mr. Tully was in his fifty-third year.

William Mower's first job was as a publican for a James Allen, "better known as Dismal Jemmy on account of his doleful aspect and lugubrious articles." Allen was the "reporter and subeditor of the *Adelaide Times,*" and by 1850, he had created "South Australia's first comic magazine" the *Monthly Almanac and Illustrated Commentator,* in which he employed William Mower as "the main writer of parodies and puns." In 1850, he also joined the local amateur dramatic society, the Adelaide Garrick Club, where he was the secretary. The *South Australian Register* in 1853 noted the success of one of his first Australian musical farces, *Quite Colonial,* performed by the Nelson family, which was reputed to be "quite a hit" by "all who witnessed the first representation."

In the same year, the *Adelaide Observer* told of William Mower's kindness in the article "Australian Benevolence":

> A short time ago attention was called to the case of the widow of the late Mr. T. H. Thompson, who was situated in circumstances of peculiar distress. Mr. Thompson had been for a time engaged upon the Adelaide press, but removed to Melbourne, where he obtained an excellent

> situation upon the Argus newspaper. There his health declined, and he determined to return to this colony, to take possession of an easier, but still remunerative appointment. His illness increased, and he died upon the voyage, leaving a widow who landed in a state of destitution; for his long and distressing malady had wasted his means. She was almost unknown here, and must have sought refuge in the Destitute Asylum, had it not been for the active benevolence of Mr. W. M. Akhurst, a gentleman also connected with the press, who had formerly been acquainted with her husband. Hearing of her distress, he exerted himself to raise a subscription on her behalf; and Mrs. Akhurst showed much personal kindness to her and her little orphans. He was successful beyond his most sanguine expectations collecting over £120.

After working in the *Free Press* for six months, that journal folded.

In the outer world, two sparks occurred in Australia in 1851 that set Victoria on fire, and by 1854, Melbourne was a city rising rapidly in prosperity. The first trigger had been the separation of the colony of Victoria from NSW, and the second was the discovery of gold a few months later in the newly launched colony. Over this period, the population of the colony had quadrupled, so that "by the end of 1854 it exceeded that of New South Wales." The year 1854 was a monumental time for Victoria with the infamous Eureka Stockade on the Ballarat Goldfields, the opening of the University of Melbourne, the opening of the Melbourne Museum, and the first edition of *The Age* newspaper. Victoria basked in the nickname "the Golden Colony."

During 1854, the family decided to move to Melbourne, in the colony of Victoria. It would be their home for the next seventeen years, whilst the final seven children would be born and christened in and around Fitzroy and Collingwood, the suburbs where they settled.

There were no reporters to greet them.

William Akhurst's show business activities soon blossomed in their new situation, and within three years, the newspaper reporters had found him!

Following are three typical indications of the successes he enjoyed for his writings for the Melbourne stage:

In an article written in *The Age* from January 1857:

> On Saturday night, Mr W. M. Akhurst, the author of the Pantomime, took his benefit; we trust it is a good one. He deserves it, for a Pantomime of twenty nights' run in the colonies, is indeed something to talk about

Another article in *The Age* from January 1858:

> A new Pantomime entitled "Harlequin Whittington, and his Cat," written by Mr W. M. Akhurst, has enjoyed great popularity at the Theatre Royal ever since Christmas, and we suppose will not be withdrawn till the audiences become very much smaller than they are at present.

And in the *Sydney Morning Herald* from January 1859:

> The Theatre Royal has been crowded for the last two nights. "Harlequin Robin Hood, or the Wild Huntsman of Sherwood," the latest production of that versatile genius, Mr W. Akhurst, has been a great success. The theatrical critics are unanimous in their judgement, and so are the pit, boxes, and gallery. The piece is brim full of wit, and the local allusions are most telling. There is no savagery. The satire is genuine good humour, and those whom it touches, although, like the tight trousered boy at "rounders," compelled to rub, are bound to admit that it was all done in "fair play."

In Melbourne, William Mower really came into his own as a journalist for *The Argus* and "as a burlesque writer for the stage." Some of the quirky exotic titles of his works include ones where he was credited as the adaptor, such as *Romance and Reality or, The Digger in London* (1854); *L'Africaine or, The Fickle Geographer and the Fair Aboriginal* (1866); ones where he was credited as the playwright, such as *The Battle of Melbourne or, A Column Wanted* (1854); *King Arthur or, Launcelot the Loose; Gin-ever the Square and the Knights of the Round Table and Other Furniture* (1868), and *The Battle of Hastings or, The Duke, the Earl, the Witch, the Why, and the Wherefore* (1869) and as a writer, as in *The Rights of Woman* (1854).

The stage is fickle, and while the1850s had proven to be a highly successful decade for him with his move to Melbourne and its theatre scene, the 1860s brought him a new set of troubles. In 1860, William Mower filed a lawsuit against a Mr Brooke and the management of the Theatre Royal "for breach of contract, in not employing him to write the Christmas pantomime," in which "the damages claimed were £80." This situation was resolved when he received a benefit from Mr Brooke at the Theatre Royal to recover that loss. Then in 1866, he was declared insolvent as seen in the following excerpt:

> William Mower Akhurst, of Fitzroy, journalist. Causes of insolvency—Want of employment, and pressure of creditors. Liabilities, £120 11s. 6d. assets, £25; deficiency, £95 11s 6d.
> E Courtney, official assignee

However, difficulties aside, perhaps his most glorious performance came in January 1868, when Prince Alfred, Duke of Edinburgh, son of Queen Victoria, visited Melbourne. He was entertained at an evening performance of William Mower's "deservedly popular pantomime" *Tom, Tom, the Piper's Son and Mary, Mary Quite Contrary,* which was reportedly performed "with great success to a crowded house."

William Mower (Akhurst) and Ellen had thirteen children:

- Ellen Florence (1846–1847), died aged ten months.
- Francis William (1847–1848), died aged one year.
- Adrian Charles (1848–1927) married Christina Mitchell, and together they had nine children. In 1909, he was living at Shoobra Rd, Elsternwick, Victoria, and working as a clerk. He died in Manly, NSW.
- Arthur William (1851–1907) was born in Adelaide, South Australia. He married Marion Elizabeth White Robertson in England in 1876. In 1881, she filed for divorce from him citing "adultery coupled with desertion for upwards of two years without reasonable excuse." According to his 1881 English census record, Arthur William was then married secondly to Charlotte, and with

her had a son, also called Arthur. But by 1891, both of them had died. Passing reference was made that one of the Arthurs was an actor.

- *Sidney Philip Akhurst was not newsworthy. He is often regaled in our family for his marriage to the German, Alice Kitz. Their daughter of the same name, Alice, became Alice McFadzean upon marriage to Frederick Lamont McFadzean, and as Judy's grandparents, the rest is history.*
- Walter Frederick (1854–1904) married Kate Deutsch. He was born in Adelaide and died in Newtown, Victoria.
- William James (1855–1857) was born in North Melbourne and died in Victoria aged one year.
- Ellen Florence (1856–?) was born in East Melbourne. She left Australia with her parents in 1870 for England, where she married Walter Henry Chapman in 1893.
- William Howard (1858–1872) was born in Collingwood. He died in Victoria at the age of twelve.
- Sophia Maria (1859–1860) was born in Collingwood. She died in Victoria.
- Thomas Carlyle (1861–1934) was born in Collingwood. He married Emilia Napthaly in Sydney in 1885, and they had at least four children. He worked as a clerk.
- Victor Hugo (1863–?) was born in Fitzroy. He travelled back to England in 1870 with his parents.
- Oscar James (1864–1940) was born in Fitzroy. He married Jessie Florence Smith, and together they had approximately three children, one of whom was tennis player Daphne Jessie Akhurst.

End Days

In 1870, William Mower, Ellen, and a couple of his family travelled back to London aboard the *Kent*. It has been speculated that his choice to leave Australia was driven by ambition for success in England like the success he had experienced in Australia. Though the life of William Mower and Ellen in England is relatively unknown, he did not have the same success there as he had in Australia.

William Mower died due to a "paralysis of the brain" in June 1878, aged fifty-five, aboard the *Patriarch* en route back to Australia from London. He was buried at sea, and his widow, Ellen, returned to Australia alone. As a result of her husband's untimely death, Ellen was "left in very poor circumstances," so in March 1879, "an amateur performance, tendered by the members of the Melbourne press" was organised for her benefit. The performance took place attended by the governor.

Ellen Akhurst died in Melbourne, Victoria, in 1915. A notice marking her death was written in the *Leader* newspaper and reads as follows:

> Deaths—On the 18th August, at 26 Moore Street, St Kilda, Ellen, relict of the late William Mower Akhurst, formerly of Melbourne, dramatic author and journalist, and dearly beloved mother of Adrian Charles and Sidney Philip Akhurst of Melbourne, and Thomas Carlyle and Oscar James Akhurst of Sydney, in her 94th year.

It only remains to end this chapter with an account of the character of the Akhurst founding father down-under, William Mower Akhurst, as written by his contemporaries in his 1878 obituary:

> Old colonists will well remember his genial social qualities, amiable disposition, and kindly nature, that never made him an enemy; his infinite jest and ready humour, that used to "set the table in a roar"; and they will give a sigh to the memory of "Poor Akhurst," to whom glad life seemed so sweet and joyous a boon.

Johann Ludwig Kitz: "The Germanic Link"

During the late 1800s, it was not surprising for the British upper class to have German links. In 1837, George IV's niece, who also had a partly German bloodline, was crowned Queen Victoria. She went on to marry her cousin the German Prince Albert of Saxe-Coburg and Gothe.

In 1820, Johann Ludwig Kitz was born in the German town of Hanau, known as a fairy-tale town because it is the birthplace of the Grimm brothers. It is situated just east of the city of Frankfurt, and since the sixteenth century, Hanau has been renowned as a "centre of the jewel and precious-metal trade." The Kitz family showed a preference for these trades. The primary religion of Hanau was Calvinism.

Johann Ludwig Kitz, who went by Louis, spent the first nineteen years of his life in Germany. Whilst Louis's parents remain unknown, he did have a younger brother, Carl Jacob Kitz (1828–1892), who was a jewel-case maker

In 1839, Louis left Germany via Hamburg for England aboard the *Countess of Lonsdale,* arriving in London on November 6. On the ship's record, his occupation was listed as "Watchmaker," and he soon found work in London in this profession. He anglicised his name to Lewis. The shipping records suggest that sometime between 1841 and 1843, he had gone back to Germany. He returned to London via Rotterdam aboard the *Columbine* on April 9, 1843.

In the meantime, Carl followed his older brother to live in England, where he remained for the rest of his life. In 1856, he married a Miss Ellen Blake, and together they had four known children—Minnie (1864–1948), Carl Adolphe (1865–1953), John Christopher (1869–1927), and James Louis (1870–1946).

The Kitz Family

In early 1842, Louis married Jane Mortimer Jeffery (1821–1886) in London. Jane was born in Kirton, Devon, and was baptised at Kenton, Devon, on December 11, 1821. Jane's origins are a little unclear though according to an 1841 census, it seems that she had a sister, Rebecca, who was twelve years younger sister.

Louis and Jane Kitz spent the first years of their married life in London, where Louis continued to work as a watchmaker. Their first four children were born in London. Their eldest daughter, Emma Jane, died at approximately age five years of convulsions. In 1851, they were living on Maddox Street in St George Hanover Square, before visiting Hanau, Germany, in 1852, where their fifth child and second son, Charles William, was born. They returned to London in September 1852 aboard the *Ocean*.

Altogether, Louis and Jane had ten children:

- John Louis Kitz (1843–?) was born on May 9 and baptised in Westminster on June 25. He migrated to Australia with his parents in 1853.
- Emma Jane Kitz (1845–1850) was born and died in London, England. She died in convulsions.
- Ellen Kitz (1847–1928) was born in London and migrated to Australia with her parents. On November 14, 1868, she married John Feridoline Charles Brache at St Paul's Church in Geelong. Brache was originally from Coblentz-on-the-Rhine, Prussia, and together they had approximately six children: Jane Eliza (1869–?), Carl Coblenz (1871–1941), Albert Ernest (1872–?), Ellen Alice (1874–1874), Eliza Ernestine (1875–?), and Dorothea Olga (1883–?).
- Mathilda Kitz (1850–?) was born in London and migrated to Australia in 1853.
- Charles William Kitz (1852–1896) was born in Hanau, Germany. He married Louisa Norman on January 6, 1877. He was a wine merchant and a senior partner in L. Kitz and Sons, past Senior Grand Warden of the Grand Lodge of Freemasons of Victoria, and representative of the Grand Lodge of NSW. He died on July 5, 1896, at North-Brighton, Victoria. In his will, all his property was left to his brother, Paul Julius, except his furniture and jewellery, which was left to his widow.
- Frederick George Kitz (1855–1931) was born in Melbourne. He worked as a wine merchant. He married Margaret Emily Heron in 1891, and they had two daughters—Evelyn May (1892–1942) and Emily Vera (1894–?)—and possibly a third called Dorothy Winifred.
- Caroline Jane Kitz (1857–1901) was born in Victoria. In 1880, she was admitted to the Kew Asylum. She died in Sunbury Lunatic Asylum.
- *Alice Kitz (1859–1921) married Sidney Phillip Akhurst and thus become Judy's great-grandmother through their eldest daughter, Alice Edith Akhurst, who had four siblings.*

- Paul Julius Kitz (1862–1918) was born in Geelong and died in Melbourne. He married heiress Georgina Watson in 1891. They had a son, also called Paul Julius Kitz.
- Theodore Kitz (1864–1869) was born in Geelong.

The Australian Gold Rush

The Kitz family—parents Louis and Jane, and their children Lewis Jr, Ellen, Mathilda, and Charles William—departed from Dartmouth for Australia aboard the *Barrackpore* in December 1852. They arrived in Melbourne ninety-four days later, in February 1853. The voyage was described in the local newspaper as "a pleasant passage." Given the timing of their arrival in Victoria, their decision to live in the Geelong District, and Louis's later employment as a miner on the Steiglitz goldfields, it is almost certain that the gold rush was the prime motivator for the family's decision to come to Australia. Gold was discovered in Victoria in 1851, and the Kitzes were part of the 90,000 people who travelled to Victoria in 1852.

Once again Louis Kitz's first employment in Australia was as a watchmaker and jeweller in Geelong. He knew advertising would never go astray, and a few months after the Kitz family's arrival in Australia, the following notice was placed by Louis in the *Geelong Advertiser and Intelligencer* on April 16, 1853:

> Louis Kitz, Watch and Clock Maker, Jeweller, from Regent Street, begs to inform the inhabitants of Ashby and the surrounding neighbourhood, that he has opened a shop in the above line in Candover-Street, near the New Church, where he hopes by strict attention to business, and moderate charges, to merit their support and patronage.

Eureka! The Call of Gold

Louis's eyes turned to gold even though he had a successful watchmaking business in Geelong, first on Candover Street and later on Moorabool Street, which was one of the main streets in the CBD. Halfway between Ballarat and Geelong, on Sutherland Creek, alluvial gold had been discovered in

1853, and this encouraged a small town to spring up at Steiglitz. The name came from the von Steiglitz family who, "were the first European settlers to establish a run in the area in 1847." As is normal, the alluvial gold started to run out, but the discovery of auriferous (gold-bearing) quartz in 1855 established the town's permanence for the ensuing decades.

The first record of Louis living in Steiglitz was in 1855, when the local newspaper described the discovery of quartz in Steiglitz:

> A new and extensive reef of auriferous quartz has been struck, about a mile to the N.E. of the late rich discovery. It has been christened Sailor's Reef, and has been traced about two miles, one half of which extent has been marked oft. Mr Kitz, our respected townsman, brought samples of the auriferous quartz to the 'Advertiser Office,' last evening, which by their richness promises well.

Louis was particularly involved in the mining of auriferous quartz at Steiglitz. And with the touch of an entrepreneur, it was Louis who went on to "import the first quartz-crushing machinery into the colony" in 1856. An 1856 report on the Steiglitz Quartz Crushing Company reported his success:

> In the meantime, Kitz's machine crushes about double the quantity of any other [quartz] on the gold field, and generally averages about double in gold returns. He has obtained another contract from Davis's party to crush the remainder of their quartz or part of it, and consequently will be occupied busily for months to come. In the course of another week the machine of the Steiglitz Quartz Crushing Company will have obtained its additional set of rollers, and if the expectations entertained in regard to its operations be not over sanguine, Mr. Kitz has need to look to his laurels. These two machines, and those of the Steiglitz Gold Quartz Crushing Company, and Mr. Love's may be said to be the principal machines on the diggings.

In 1867, Louis was voted one of seven directors of the New Alliance Quartz Mining Company, Steiglitz with the most votes of thirty-one, indicating, not only his great investment in, but also considerable success with quartz crushing in Steiglitz.

Colonial Wine Merchant

While Louis Kitz began as a watchmaker in Germany and England, and later as a miner on the Victorian goldfields, he was primarily remembered by his peers as a wine merchant and the first man to enter the colonial wine business. Whilst it is not known precisely when he entered the wine trade (possibly 1856), it was sometime before 1862 as in that year he was presented with a silver cup "by the wine-growers of the Geelong district, in token of their esteem for his laudable exertions in promoting the colonial wine trade." In 1862, he also purchased the Ceres Vineyard, located on the Barrabool Hills, which he bought for "70 pounds per acre including all improvements." Louis had a reputation as "one of the largest Melbourne buyers of colonial wine," and a buyer of the Murray vintage in particular.

He returned to his cider making. In 1883, it was reported in the *Weekly Times* that "Mr. Kitz, the well-known colonial wine merchant, has commenced cider-making at Brighton from apples." During his lifetime, he did not have as much success with cider as with wine as he found, "the right sort of apples were not grown in Victoria," but he "encouraged fruit growers to grow the proper kind of apples, by showing them that cider could be made in Victoria, even with the apples they had."

Kitz Cider.

Family Tragedies

Brighton became the area of choice for many members of the Kitz family to live, and Louis's wife, Jane, died there of cancer in 1886, aged sixty-five years. Some of the Kitz children met with misfortunes. Youngest son Theodore died in Brighton aged five years. Eldest son John Louis was a "steady, intelligent lad," a student at Geelong Grammar School, who accidently fell down some stairs that led to a permanent head injury rendering him "insane." He was looked after in Yarra Bend Asylum, "suffering from a form of insanity tending to dementia or absolute loss of mind, acute mania, and, fixed delusions." Similarly, daughter Caroline Jane also suffered some kind of mental deficiency or dementia and was placed in Kew Asylum in 1880. She died at age forty-four in Sunbury Lunatic Asylum.

Son Frederick George was involved in the 1881 Jolimont Railway accident. *The Riverine Grazier* reported:

> The six minutes to nine express from Brighton, which, after leaving Balaclava, travels without stopping to Flinders street, was the subject of a terrible catastrophe. The train consisted of nine carriages and a brake van, the latter following the engine. Nothing unusual attracted attention until after passing through Richmond station, when a series of bumps were felt. When the engine reached the Jolimont crossing, the tire of the fore wheel on the right hand side of the fifth carriage fractured between two of the spokes. At every revolution of the wheel other segments of the tire broke off, and the ends of the spokes rolled on the rails causing a rapid succession of jolting blows. About 100 yards from the Jolimont level crossing a tolerably sharp curve commences. When the disabled wheel arrived at this point it appears that the disarrangement of the position of the axle, consequent upon its depression on the broken side by the carriage spring, caused the damaged wheel to leave the rail. The broken end then ploughed into the ground and acted as a lever to throw the carriage off the track and over the embankment. The diversion of the carriage seems to have snapped the couplings of the one immediately in front, and it toppled over the bank into a muddy pool, dragging the two carriages at the rear along with it. The

> two succeeding carriages, however were carried by their momentum a few feet beyond the carriage that caused the accident. The first of the three carriages—the one with the broken wheel—was shattered to pieces, and how the occupants who were in it escaped with their lives is a perfect marvel.

Three people were killed, and twenty-two were injured. Frederick George, riding in the "second-class ordinary" carriage, was "pinioned by the leg" and had to be pulled out of the wreckage. He sustained some internal injuries and lost his leg.

End Days

Louis left Melbourne "bound for a pleasure trip to Great Britain" on April 1, 1887, aboard the *Ormuz*. For those who travel much to Scotland, it is hard to believe, but while he was there during late June, he died of sunstroke! His burial in a London cemetery was organised by his brother, Carl. For his surviving five children—Ellen, Alice, Charles William, Paul Julius, and Frederick—he left £1,960 in his will. His wine and cider business continued in the hands of his son Charles William until his death in 1896, and then by Paul Kitz until 1918. The Kitz business continued to have success.

Louis's memory is preserved in Melbourne through the name of Kitz Lane, which runs north from Little Collins Street between William and Queen Streets. He was remembered by his friends and peers as "a well-known and highly-respected colonist, against whose character no one could say a word."

CHAPTER 7

When the Saints Go Marching In

My Father is working until now and I myself am working.
—John 15:17

Always abounding in the work of the Lord.
—1 Corinthians 15:58

At the beginning of this biography, the simplest question was, "When does a biography start?" Well, 1849 would seem to be as good as any. That year was chosen as it was when William Mower Akhurst, Judy's great-great-grandfather, arrived in Adelaide, the first of her ancestors to arrive in Australia.

The question could be asked again: "When does a biography start?" The reply this time could be 1939, her birth year. I mean, the biography is about her!

As a sucker for punishment, the question could be asked again: "When does a biography start?" and the nuanced reply could be, "Around 8 p.m. on Sunday, October 4, 1957, for that was when Judy was born again, a babe in Christ.

Born Again

Two very simple words, but when used together, they have become inextricably linked to refer to spiritual rebirth, or a regeneration of the human spirit, and is contrasted with physical birth. Although parts of the following may seem a tad theological, it is integral to Judy's way of life.

The words came into their own during the English Great Awakening, which was strongest in the 1730s and 1740s. The Wesleys, along with George Whitfield, were associated with the awakening, and Whitfield was reputed to have preached on the text "You must be born again" time after time. When one of his friends asked him, "Why do you preach so often on the text 'You must be born again,'" Whitfield simply replied, "Because you must be born again."

The American D. L. Moody was another powerful evangelist. He was born in 1837. He became a Christian at eighteen and moved to Chicago. At twenty-four, he left the shoe business for good and proved to be an effective social worker among the poor. He also began undertaking evangelistic missions. He did say, "There are many better speakers than I am … but all I can say is that the Lord uses me." He was reputed to have preached on the text "You must be born again" 183 times during his campaign days.

For our generation, the evangelist has been Billy Graham. His ministry began in 1947 at the Greater Los Angeles Revival. Over sixty years, he had preached to over 200 million people through 400 crusades in 185 countries. The enthusiasm was palpable throughout the churches as Billy's April 1959 Sydney crusade drew closer. Judy came into her own as she has never been short on enthusiasm. Invitations had to be dropped off in letter boxes, strangers contacted, people organised onto buses, and so on. Her whimsy sparked when knowledge became available as to when Billy would be landing at Sydney's Kingsford Smith aerodrome. She was going to be there to welcome him. She was! It was a civilised time whereby passengers would descend the steps from the aircraft and walk across the tarmac through a waist-high fence into the Arrivals Hall. Judy was very chuffed that she shook Billy's hand to welcome him to Sydney and the crusade. (There was a running joke after this handshake in that Judy did not wash her hand for a week.)

Billy Graham never swerved from the simple, basic but imperative message that God had given him to share with the world. No man in history remained so focused on those five important words: "You must be born again!"

How does being born again work in real life? The Bible provides a basic, two-part division of humanity in that if one is not born again, one belongs to "the kingdoms of this world." If you are born again, one belongs to the kingdom of God.

What Happens at Being Born Again

If we start again with Judy, then we have, "Five foot two eyes of blue, but oh what those five foot could do, has anybody seen my gal?" So if you do see her, you can immediately say, "Yes, that's Judy." But is what you see the total Judy? Not really. There is the full package—her personality, her loves, her drives, and her hopes—that makes Judy, Judy. I can remember Ko-Ko, the antihero in Gilbert and Sullivan's *The Mikado,* watching his bride-to-be, Yum Yum, walking away philosophises and sighs, "There she goes! To think how entirely my future happiness lies in that little package." The package, also known as the person, consists of a body and a soul. The body keeps the soul in contact with the world through its five basic senses—sight, smell, taste, hearing, and touch. However, the soul is the actual real person, the person who matters to God.

Whilst the soul has contact with the world, it does not have contact with God for He is Spirit. But when God moves in a person's life, His Spirit touches the soul. This is the moment when what was born of the flesh is also been born of God's Spirit and is born again or born from above!

The effect on the body at that time is different for different personalities as exemplified by John Wesley, C. S. Lewis, and Judy.

1) On the evening of May 24, 1738, John Wesley reluctantly attended a meeting in Aldersgate. Someone read from Luther's *Preface to the Epistle to the Romans.* About 8:45 p.m., "while he was describing the change which God works in the heart through faith in Christ, I felt my heart strangely warmed. I felt I did trust in Christ, Christ alone for salvation; and an assurance was given me that He had taken away my sins, even mine, and saved me from the law of sin and death."
2) C. S. Lewis recorded, "In the Trinity Term of 1929 I gave in, and admitted that God was God and knelt and prayed. Perhaps that night, the most dejected and reluctant convert in all England."
3) In some of our later discussions, Judy would comment that she could not think of any of her ancestors who had any Christian background. Her parents, however, did think it appropriate during her childhood that both Judy and John attend Sunday school, being it was the thing to do in the then social mores. When they had settled into their newly built Seaforth home, Judy and John were taken to the Methodist Sunday school at Gilbert Park in Manly. John recounts that their attendance was not for any extended time. However, in retrospect, during the time there, the stories of Jesus were sown into her life. In one of His parables, Jesus described this to be the seed (of the Word of God), which could germinate one day. The timing of this blossoming goes back to evening classes at Fort Street High when, at the end of the last class, Judy and several others would catch the bus to Manly, getting off at the stop servicing Seaforth Public School, Frenches Forest Road. From there, Judy would take off her high-heeled shoes and run the short distance up the low rise of Ethel Street to her parents' house in Plant Street.

   On a pleasant early October bus trip home, Bob, one of the night student group, said to her, "Why don't you come down to the Bapos?" "Who were the Bapos?" Judy mused. It soon sorted itself out that they were the Baptists who worshipped a short distance down Frenches Forest Road from the bus stop.

   Judy sat alone at the evening service in the un-full Seaforth Baptist Church for it was the long Labour Day weekend, and most in her age group were away, camping in the Blue Mountains. A layman, Trevor Anthony, preached on the subject that God loved us so much that Christ died on the cross for our sins. An overwhelming conviction coursed through her: *God loves me, and Christ died for me.* As he finished his sermon, Trevor challenged anyone who wished to accept God's love to indicate, and Judy's hand went exuberantly straight up. Judy has never doubted being born again at that moment and has thrown herself into the work of the Lord.

She finds it reflective that God used Trevor Anthony for that moment in her life though she was never to meet or even see him again. This reminded Judy of the Bible's account of Philip, the evangelist, and the Ethiopian eunuch (Acts 8:26–40). They met under God's unique guidance on the desert road from Jerusalem to Gaza. Philip told him the good news about Jesus, and the eunuch was born again. Philip was then taken by an angel to around Azortus, where he continued his evangelism. After the disappearance of the evangelists, the Ethiopian and Judy went on their way into the rest of their lives, rejoicing for what the Lord had done for them.

The news immediately came up the mountains that an unknown young lady had become a Christian overnight at the church. Over sixty-six years later, Judy has not wavered from that night's commitment to make Jesus her Lord. This was evidenced when a much-loved visitor in our home was innocently playing on the piano, Frank Sinatra's song, "I did it My Way". Upon the songs completion Judy immediately rose like as an avenging force and said, "We do not play that song in this house we do it Christ's Way."

Another way of phrasing it is that she had become a pilgrim.

Born Again for Life and the Pilgrim Way

For many people, being a pilgrim carries the concept of undertaking yearly, or at least regular, walking journeys of at least several days' duration from one sacred locale to another.

The other aspect is that all Christians are pilgrims, and every day is to be a walk with Jesus. Two books shed much light around the subject: *The Pilgrims Progress*, published in 1678, and *In His Steps*, in 1896.

The Pilgrims Progress from This World to That Which Is to Come

The *Pilgrim's Progress* (was shortened from the title above) was written by John Bunyan, a destitute travelling tinker (a handyman in modern parlance). His wife was also destitute, and all she had to bring in her dowry to her marriage were two Christian books. Bunyan spent twelve years in prison because he would not give up preaching, which was forbidden for him as a nonconformist. During his incarceration, Bunyan wrote the book. Instead of using simple English words to help explain how Christians should avoid sinful ways to reach heaven, he turned the story into an allegory whereby their dangers were pictured as all sorts of roadblocks, such as the "Slough of Despond and the Town of Stupidity" and fearsome creatures such as "Mr Despondency," daughter "Much-Afraid," and the giant, "One Grim."

In His Steps: What Would Jesus Do?

What Would Jesus Do? (was shortened from the title above) was written by Charles M. Sheldon, who had become a minister of the Central Congregational Church of Topeka, Kansas. His weekly preaching was around societal problems, and they would be solved by working through, resolving, and applying the answer to the question, "What would Jesus do?" In due course, the weekly sermons were turned into a Christian novel set in the fictional First Church of Raymond. It starts with a homeless man breaking into a church service and asking for help. The congregation's response was underwhelming. Yet the minister, Henry Maxwell, mused that for the comfortable routine of First Church, life would never be the same for the apathetic congregation. For the just over 125 years on the market, the reputed book sales have been around 50,000,000 copies.

From the sublime to the ridiculous, the following Syndal Church newsletter Editorials provide other aspects of being followers of Jesus—a pilgrim people.

Vol. 35, No. 5 Sunday, 2 February 1992

A Pilgrim People (1)
(or perhaps a mansion just over the hilltop)

Let me confess, but then all older married ladies already know that there are naughty boys ready to break out from older men. Thus, it will be no surprise that the other day when I was working Mildura alone, I was happily watching *Indiana Jones and the Last Crusade* on the TV without she-who-must-be-obeyed telling me to show some maturity. Normally a sigh can say an awful lot.

Anyway, there was Indiana and his father in Berlin in the middle of a Nazi rally, during which the father simply said, "We are pilgrims in an unholy land," to which I responded to myself, "and so are all we Christians."

For those of riper years, it is not particularly hard for us to realise we are now in an unholy place since we were raised in a relatively Christian society where right was right and wrong was wrong.

Yet, even when it seems the best of times, as Jesus recognised, the devil is the prince of this world (John 14:30), and the Prince of Power of the Air (Eph. 2:2). This world is not our home; we are pilgrims passing through. The ever danger is that we want to put our roots down, to feel that we are at home. It is in this world that the devil tempts us (Matt. 4:1-20).

But those that belong to God admit that they are aliens and strangers on earth. People who say such things show that they are looking for a country, a heavenly one. Therefore, God is not ashamed to be called their God for he has prepared a city for them (Heb. 11:13–16).

Bob Killick

PS: "Lord, am I making You ashamed?"

....

Vol. 35, No. 6 Sunday, 9 February 1992

A Pilgrim People (2)
(or, let's get this show on the road)

Having admitted last week that I snuck in a viewing of an Indiana Jones film, let me start this week by noting that I loathe Westerns. Like all generalisations, there is often at least one exception. In my case, it is a happy little film called *The Hallelujah Trail*, which tells of the Women's Temperance Movement, led by the redoubtable Mrs Cora Templeton Massingale, to stop a wagon train of whisky reaching that sin-soaked city of Denver in the late 1800s.

Yes, the ladies win; yes, the hero and heroine marry at the end, for, "those were the days, oh pioneer west, the days of the Hallelujah Trail!" And that is the secret of being a pilgrim!

Firstly, we are on this trail as the scriptures encourage us that as Christians, we have "the way of holiness, from which even the simple need not err" (Isa. 35:8–10). The road to Sydney is nicely tarred, but out-bush there are still trails of dust made hard by those who have gone before that lead off to the horizon. We have signposts in the Bible and a plethora of Christian books offering advice from other pilgrims.

Secondly, it is the *Hallelujah* Trail. There are those who tell me I harp on the need to be a thankful people, to which I can only respond, so does the Bible! There is that plaintive query from Jesus: "Ten were healed … where are the nine? … only this foreigner has returned to give praise to God" (Luke 17:11–19). There is the challenge from Paul: "This is the *will of God,* that we give *thanks* in all circumstances" (1 Thess. 5:18; emphasis added).

Bob Killick

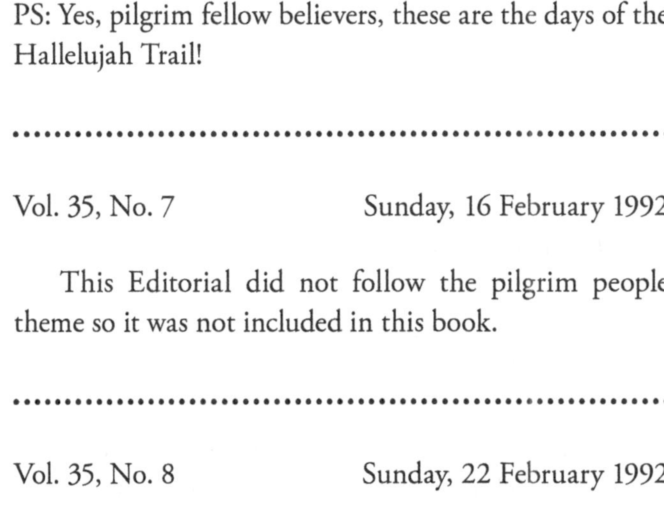

PS: Yes, pilgrim fellow believers, these are the days of the Hallelujah Trail!

....

Vol. 35, No. 7 Sunday, 16 February 1992

This Editorial did not follow the pilgrim people theme so it was not included in this book.

....

Vol. 35, No. 8 Sunday, 22 February 1992

A Pilgrim People (4)
(or bandits at twelve o'clock high)

I suppose it is a question of how your fancy takes you, but to me, there is a morbid fascination when one has arrived at one's destination to determine what has been left behind. The last time I reached Sydney, I was shy a couple of shirts and most of my reading matter. This included my compact version of John Bunyan's *Pilgrim's Progress* written, would you believe, in 1677. This is a book that I believe should be read by all Christians once a year.

For those of us who aim to make this a year of pilgrimage, it is worthwhile reviewing places where we can expect difficulties. For Pilgrim, Bunyan provided quaint but descriptive titles—the Vanity Fair of the world, the Valley of Death, Doubting Castle with Giant Despair, the Enchanted Ground, and the Silver Mine, to name a few.

We must expect Satan and his demons to attack. Pilgrim did fall and did get out of the way. By God's grace, Pilgrim was brought back onto "the way." It's interesting that Bunyan never talked about being filled by the Spirit. The euphemism he uses is, "and Pilgrim went on his way rejoicing!" We have the chorus which reminds us that "Joy is the flag flown high from the castle of our heart when the King is in residence there."

Bob Killick

PS: Let me know from your singing that you are on the Hallelujah Trail.

....

After Birth Comes Growth, Especially Spiritual Growth

At the time when the Holy Spirit came to touch Judy, the Spirit gave her the gift of faith, and she became a Christian, that is to be born again or born from above. At that moment, and like everyone else who is born again, the Spirit endowed her with those Spiritual gifts or graces that He had chosen for her. Each person receives at least one, and their only purpose, then as now, is for the building up of the church. These spiritual gifts or graces are described in three major groupings in Paul's letters to Corinth (1 Cor. 12:7–11), Rome (12:3–8), and Ephesus (4:10–12). There are graces mentioned singly in both Paul's and Peter's other letters, such as, "Show Hospitality to one another without grumbling—As each has received a grace, use it to serve one another as good stewards of God's multifaceted Grace (1 Peter 4:9–10).

At a child's birthday party, there is nothing like the excitement caused by the opening of the gifts. The same anticipation occurs when the new Christian explores which gifts were endowed at conversion. These gifts develop with experiences and in time.

Faith

To be able to become a Christian, God provides everyone with the gift of a "normal and saving faith." This is so succinctly put in Ephesians 2:8–9: "For it is by grace you have been saved, through faith … it is the gift of God, not by any of our works, religious or otherwise, so that no one could boast that they had done it themselves."

The grace of faith is on another level since, for example, it is distinguished from the saving faith whereby the recipient carries the sense that God's will shall be accomplished. His will is unstoppable. As an example there was the time we were contemplating buying Victorian Chemicals, which would put us into serious debt. This did not sit well with Judy's natural Scottish instincts. She was talking through the situation with her close friend, Marjorie, when the faith words came out: "It is the Lord that provides opportunities. I think we should let Bob go ahead and buy."

Giving

Whilst most Christians are givers to the Lord's work, those with the grace of giving will share with extraordinary generosity. Two examples of the styles of giving are shown in the New Testament. The first example is in 1 Corinthians 13:5, where it is stated that "Love keeps no record of wrongs." The parallel to this is that when the grace of giving is being undertaken, "an extraordinary giver keeps no score of what is being given now or has been over the years."

The second characteristic of an extraordinary giver is that he or she thinks ahead. The immediate act of the Good Samaritan was to arrange for the man who fell among thieves to be settled into the inn. In the morning, the next step was to give the innkeeper two silver coins along with the now noteworthy instruction, "Look after him and when I return, I will reimburse you for any extra expense you may have had" (Luke 10:35). This is the action of a giver extraordinaire.

Mercy and Helping

Judy has the grace of mercy possessing a ministry of visitation, prayer, and compassion to and for those in need. The grace of helping others links with mercy, and the possessor of this grace has a spiritual burden and a God-given love for the needy and afflicted. It is not rare to have Judy shedding tears for the afflicted ones, and her ministry remains tireless.

On the day before Beth, one of Judy's dear friends, died, Judy had visited her in the nursing home and prayed over her while she slept soundly. Our care pastor wrote to Judy a week later:

> Dear Judy (and Bob), July 2018
>
> Thank you *ever* so much for being the hands, feet and heart of Jesus to Beth and her family. You were the *best* possible carers from Syndal for Beth and her family and I am in awe of your capacity to care for Beth in the midst of concert preparations and festivities.
>
> I am so blessed to belong to this church with you in it!
>
> You have such a unique and extensive way of caring for soooooo many people at both the 1:1 level and at the more "corporate" level. Your capacity to care astounds me, and your additional contributions to the life and ministries of SBC are equally spectacular! You have already left a legacy that most people would only dream of leaving. Your generosity of time, energy, thoughtfulness, resources, and compassionate care are soooo inspiring!!!! The Spirit of God is evident in you.
>
> I often thank God for you and greatly value your kindness and regular encouragements.
>
> Love from Lyn

Hospitality

Hospitality is as old as humanity and has modified itself as the world and circumstances have changed over the centuries. What started with an extra room in a house slowly metamorphosed to the earliest inns, staging posts, and hotels to the modern motels and holiday resorts of today. In Australia's 2017 Treasury figures, what is now known as the hospitality industry had just over $53 billion passing through its hands. Hospitality is the way we treat people who are away from home. Staying at an inn during biblical times was both costly and dangerous since they were known as hangouts for prostitutes and thieves, and the traveller depended on the kindness of normal folks. With the flow of Christians on the move after the formation of the early church, the members of the newly forming fellowships were encouraged to be a hospitable people looking to aid the itinerant evangelists.

Judy has been extraordinarily hospitable throughout her life. A brief mention of some of her actions include: helping settle under the supervision of Deaconess Doris Fletcher, known affectionately as "Mum," the many Vietnamese refugees during the 1980s influx of boat people; hosting groups of students for a meal and fellowship; using our home for many years for the regular monthly Saturday Homemakers group; running small-group weekly Bible studies for around a dozen participants; providing accommodations for overseas (such as Papua New Guinea, the United Kingdom, and the United States) mission visitors for up for a week or so; running and providing morning weekly Bible studies for a ladies' fellowship gathering; monthly post-Sunday evening services for hymn singing with Judy playing organ and piano. The regular Sunday meals for new people/visitors at the church have been Judy's pièce de résistance. Her eagle-eye scanned the congregation, entering and exiting, to determine who she might ask for the meal. Sometimes bookings were made into the future; and providing afternoon teas for the neighbours to maintain contact with each other.

> Long-term accommodation hospitality has the most challenges with both their, and our, foibles on show. Our longest-staying guest of going on two years was a friend of Andrew's from the country and gave for our annals the great brussels sprouts fiasco. In contrast, when we are just *en famille*, when there are visitors, there is always pressure as to what should be on the menu. Judy always believes in expanding the choice, and so amongst "the greens," the brussels sprouts made their appearance. Our new friend seemed to enjoy them, whereas our children let their mum know quietly that the sprouts could be left off their plates. The climax was reached the night when all the sprouts ended up on the friend's plate. "But I don't like them,"

and they never appeared again We all had a good laugh, and it reinforced that, with hospitality, a sense of humour is worth its weight in gold.

Teaching

Teaching is teaching. One can be a most talented teacher as the result of genetic inheritance and training. The grace of teaching given by the Spirit will be evidenced within the natural teaching world, but its main use is God's truths in the Spiritual kingdom. It was Jesus, in John 10:11, 27, who could say, "I am the Good Shepherd … My sheep hear my voice … they follow me." When taught by one graced by the Spirit, listeners can sense that they are hearing as if from the Good Shepherd Himself.

In the earlier years of our married life, Judy was fully involved in the raising of our growing brood, which left Bible study meetings for the evenings. Judy enjoyed these mixed cell groups and was always enmeshed in the discussions although she did not think it appropriate to take over the leadership.

For the fifty years in Melbourne, she has been able to lead a ladies' Bible study held in our home. Most of the studies came from the Melbourne Branch of the Christian Ladies' Fellowship.

Evangelism

In the meantime, Judy soon saw that her role in life was to witness to others what the Lord had done for her. Evangelists are those who devote themselves to the presentation of the gospel.

For a brief diversion, it is worth reviewing the history of the expression "pocket battleships." This was a derisive term used during the Second World War by the British press to disparage the Deutschland class of cruisers. The German press promoted them as unsinkable, and their distinguishing feature was their large twenty-eight-centimetre (eleven-inch) calibre guns. The best remembered was the legendary Admiral Graf Spee. Because of Judy's petite size and her determined evangelistic spirit, she was soon granted the honorific title of our "pocket evangelist."

During our courting days, we participated each Saturday night at the Open Air Meeting on the Manly Corso towards the corner of Darley Road. Judy still today carries tracts in her purse and can pull them out and give one to a listener faster than a gunslinger can pull his gun from its holster. She played this role at the meetings, skirting around the back of the crowds and giving out the tracts as people would be slinking away into the darkness.

Whenever an opportunity arose, Judy would organise evangelistic outreaches in our home. It was a simple format, a cup of tea followed by the testimony of a keynote speaker. The outreach had its *moment de gloire* the day Judy arranged for Robert Colman, a keen Christian actor/singer, to attend. He was in town playing the key role in the musical comedy *Irene* during September-October 1974 at Her Majesty's Theatre. Everybody in our immediate neighbourhood had been invited, and the best count was seventy mostly ladies squeezed into the lounge and dining rooms, the hall entrance, and down the hall. The meeting is still talked about to this day.

Her heart is always searching for ways to share the gospel, and where the heart is, the giving goes. The result? Evangelical ministries always have first call on the allocation of our giving.

Evangelists who visited Tasmania.
From back left—Andrew, Clary, and Graeme.
From front left—Judy, Jenny, and Bill.

Faithfulness and Fellowship with the Saints

As we come to the end of this chapter, it is interesting to linger and consider at least one statement from amongst many of what pleases Jesus. The words *faith, faithful, faithfully,* and *faithfulness* are used about 630 times in the NIV Bible. In Matthew's gospel, Jesus gives the parable of Himself, the Master, going away on business and leaving His servants with money to look after the estate. On His return, two of the three reported they had run the business well to which the Master commended each, "Well done admirable and faithful servant—you have been faithful and trustworthy over a little, I will put you in charge of much. Enter the blessedness and share the joy which your Master enjoys."

Jesus does not say "famous servant," "successful servant," or "philanthropic servant." But He does say "faithful servant."

And who is the faithful servant but one who determines the mind of the Master and follows it.

Determining someone else's mind is not excessively difficult, particularly when it is written in a book. I think I could take a wild stab to determine what is in Jesus's mind if I read,

> And let us consider how to stir up one another to love and good works, not neglecting to meet together as the habit of some, but encouraging one another.

People are encouraged to work through these growth matters by becoming members of the church and living in the community together. As they sign the membership roll, there is the affirmation that they are signing up to be known and to know others. The rider is that they also sign to give their time, talents, and treasures to the church, making an eternal investment.

Judy has maintained an unbelievable faithfulness to being in the Lord's house each Sunday. The local church has remained the bulwark for spiritual health with Jesus referring to Himself as the Good Shepherd and the door to the sheepfold. Judy has belonged to only four sheepfolds during her life. The first was Seaforth Baptist, where she had been converted, and we had our early married years. We had another four years there between our two sojourns in England for the author's work for Unilever.

The second was Trinity Methodist Church, New Ferry, The Wirral, England, where we were located for two years for work. Our main activity was running a Wednesday night prayer and Bible study.

The third was at the Bromley Baptist Church, just outside the London postal zone. By British standards, the church was considered large with around four hundred members. It taught us that the larger church provides scope for wider ministries, which became of particular interest when we returned to Australia.

The fourth is the Syndal Baptist Church, where we have been worshipping for fifty-two years. The classic example has been that during the first twenty years, we did not missed one service unless it was going to Sydney for the family. In the twentieth year, our number 2 son began courting Alison, whose father was pastor at the Altona Meadows Baptist Church, and it was suggested that Judy and I should visit for the morning service and then stay on for lunch. We thought this was a legitimate excuse to miss Syndal. For the record, Peter and Alison have just celebrated their thirtieth wedding anniversary.

CHAPTER 8

She's the Girl Who Broke the (Casino) Bank at Monte Carlo

Who has despised the day of small beginnings?"

—Zechariah 4:10

Formalities

The following paragraph may be best described by the first line of Steve Allen's popular song "And this could be the start of something big." On "that" afternoon, no participant at the meeting had the imagination to envisage what lay in the future.

It was the afternoon of Thursday, 18 March 1983, and Judith Helen Killick of 14 Dallas Street, Mount Waverley, Victoria, became the registered holder of one hundred shares of the Victorian Chemical Company Proprietary Limited, numbered 25,101 to 25,200, at the face value of $2.00 each.

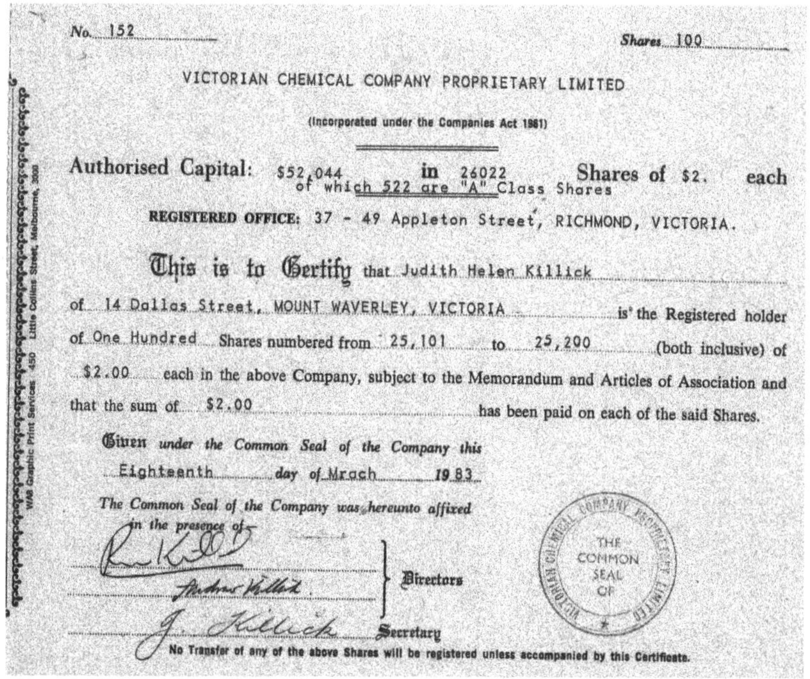

No. 152 Shares 100

VICTORIAN CHEMICAL COMPANY PROPRIETARY LIMITED

(Incorporated under the Companies Act 1961)

Authorised Capital: $52,044 in 26022 Shares of $2. each
of which 522 are "A" Class Shares

REGISTERED OFFICE: 37 - 49 Appleton Street, RICHMOND, VICTORIA.

This is to Certify that Judith Helen Killick of 14 Dallas Street, MOUNT WAVERLEY, VICTORIA is the Registered holder of One Hundred Shares numbered from 25,101 to 25,200 (both inclusive) of $2.00 each in the above Company, subject to the Memorandum and Articles of Association and that the sum of $2.00 has been paid on each of the said Shares.

Given under the Common Seal of the Company this Eighteenth day of Mrach 1983

The Common Seal of the Company was hereunto affixed in the presence of

Directors

Secretary

No Transfer of any of the above Shares will be registered unless accompanied by this Certificate.

With all the shares in their hands, a family directors' meeting was held during which Judy was appointed to the board to be company secretary, and the executive director along with the other directors Robert William Killick, Jennifer Lee Simpson, and Andrew David Killick. The family had bought the company and there might have been many cheers and much spitting. But it was modified knowing that we were only able to purchase it because Vicchem had one foot in the grave and the other on a banana skin.

The Role of a Director

There is no shortage of legal instructions on how directors should acquit themselves. Seven of them are: act honestly and carefully, know what the company is doing, take care when handling other people's money, make sure the company can pay its debts, ensure that proper financial records are kept, act in the company's best interests, and use any information gained through the director's position properly and ethically.

The choice of a director depends on his or her expertise melding with the role in the company that needs to be covered. The company could be looking for a person entitled managing, executive, finance, sales, marketing, operations, human resources, production, and IT.

An aphorism is to have a great truth summarised in a few simple words. For example, Saint Augustine (AD 354–430), bishop of Hippo, succinctly stated, "Love God and do what you wilt!" A misquote variation for a company director might be, "Be honest, and go for success!" And little did Judy know what success could be and indeed become!

Odd-Man Hypothesis

To provide an understanding of the broad impact that Judy's role gave to Vicchem over the years, it is helpful to linger on the Odd-Man Hypothesis.

The Odd-Man Hypothesis was first put forward as such by Michael Crichton in his sci-fi novel *The Andromeda Strain* (1969). Crichton had been a prolific popular author, and included in his output were *Jurassic Park* and *Rising Sun*. The plot of *Andromeda* lies in a rampant, extraterrestrial, deadly, crystalline microorganism that had been brought to earth on a crashing military satellite following a collision with a meteor. Five scientists work in "Wildfire," a specialty laboratory designed to investigate such organisms. Four of the scientists have been chosen for their brilliance. They were Jeremy Stone, the leader of the team, professor of bacteriology at Stanford, and winner of the Nobel Prize the preceding year; Peter Leavitt, clinic microbiologist who had seen more than enough plagues and epidemics to know the importance of quick action; Charles Barton, pathologist, called "The Stumbler" partly because of his talent for tumbling by error into one important discovery after another; Christian Kirke, the anthropologist from Yale with a superbly logical brain but unavailable because he's in hospital with appendicitis. Stone knew he was going to miss that kind of brain whilst his opinion of the fifth man was that he was of no value. The fifth man, Mark Hall, was a practicing surgeon and not involved in research. However, the authorities forced his inclusion to the team as the compromise candidate to cover the "odd-man" position, which was required by the protocols that allowed the authorities to build Wildfire. This hypothesis claimed that unmarried men are better able to execute the best and most dispassionate decisions in a crisis, which, of course, did eventuate in the novel.

Whilst *The Andromeda Strain* is fiction, companies are always looking for staff that has creative flair. This is also called "out-of-the-box-thinking." Sadly, those with high levels of expertise in their fields carry with them a self-importance that can create black spots in their creativity. It has therefore become more reasoned that, when looking for the creative spirit, it does not go astray to look for the "odd man" who, for example, doesn't know he's not supposed to ask certain questions!!"

A typical story of the unexpected started in 1588, when the first biscuits had been employed as rations in the British Navy. In 1847, the first chocolate bars were sold in the United Kingdom, yet it was not until the late 1930s before Mrs. Ruth Wakefield, owner of the Toll House Inn in Whitman, Massachusetts, added broken chocolate to biscuit batter thinking they would melt together in the baking. Why not, since "everyone" knew that chocolate melts at body temperature, so it will be just a mess when baking is done at around 170°C. However, against all the odds, the lady had produced the first chocolate chip biscuit.

It's Panache

In the novel, neither Mark, the Odd-Man Out, nor his colleagues recognised his value to the job that was soon to be at hand. Similarly for Judy over the years, most of her compatriots did not appreciate the panache she would provide Vicchem in the future years. Panache is not a word readily used in today's ordinary conversation, but for Judy, it is a quiet yet flamboyant confidence of style and manner. For her, it was simply doing what comes naturally, and being a person's person, she comes sparking on all cylinders into every meeting, no matter what level of management or directorship is present. Following are several vignettes that although brief, call up episodes from Judy's times working at meetings.

Call Up Sophisticates

A lobster meal.

The picture above has us at the lobster meal with other seafood delicacies to which we are being regaled by Bill (left front) and Eric (rear, under painting.) Eric was head of the Benelux section of a major European multinational enterprise. The small restaurant seated no more than twenty diners and was aimed at sophisticates even down to the use of bibs big enough to be aprons. The area had been built over the river Senne of Brussels, where the fishermen used to land their catches. I challenged Judy to eat the lobster which I thought she didn't like. But she immediately reacted, "Nonsense. I love lobster. It's just that we can't afford it." Anyway, Judy could talk the back leg off a dog, and the meal opened a good future business opportunity.

Purchase of Victorian Chemicals Factory and Business

It was easy to suggest that we would just purchase Vicchem; it was quite another matter to find $390,330 when the family could only see $15,676 cash. There was going to have to be some heavy borrowing. During the time of the money chase, Judy chatted with her lady friends about the vicissitudes of life, and one of the ladies suggested that the husbands should meet. There was interest from the other family, and they suggested lending us $50,000 but wanted a controlling shareholding. This was not what Judy envisaged. She wanted a family company controlled and run by the family. Providentially, the required loan money came through a solicitor's mortgagee's trust account, and there was no demand by them to have a controlling shareholding. The one rule was to pay the interest on time!

Purchase of the Coolaroo Site and Factory

The background was simple. The family bought Vicchem after the previous owners' fifty-year use on its Richmond site, which was distinguishable as, in the kindest words, a pile of junk. We had to move on or die as a viable production unit and really, thus our company. The light on the horizon was that the German-based Cognis was to close its Coolaroo production site. After extensive negotiations with Tony Popper, the Australia-wide director of Cognis, Vicchem was to have one chance to convince Helmut Heyman, the third-highest worldwide decision-maker of Cognis, to sell to us during his upcoming visit to Melbourne.

The photo shows from left, Judy, Helmut, Tony, and the author.

A bird in Helmut's German hand is worth two in Tony's Australian hand.

The family laid down rules about how we were to behave during the visit. It was interesting that lunch was kept to the simplicity of plates of sandwiches. Because of our family's jocular nature, it was stressed that there should be no humour when Helmut was present as Germans are a seriously minded people. Whilst the factory tour was underway Bob, discerned a twinkle in Helmut's eye and dropped the mildest quip. The result was the factory touring party blanched. However, Helmut came out of the water like a trout to a lure and said, "Yes, in Germany we tell how the husband who is under the table has his frau tell him, 'Come out from under there, and show the world you are at least in control!'" I wouldn't describe it as the best joke we had heard, but we all laughed, and the circus was now in town. Judy worked the table well with Helmut being fully caught up with family and personal matters for most of the meal. There finally followed words worth millions of dollars. Then quietly, Helmut said to Tony, "I don't see why we can't offer the sale of Coolaroo to Bob, do you Tony?" And Vicchem was on its way. It had all been a touch of perfection from the woman of gold.

Judy's other touch during the purchase of Coolaroo was as the negotiations got underway with Coolaroo's senior management, there was a push by an insider management trio who also dreamt of taking over the site. The basis of their promotion was that they would provide the manufacture, whilst we had all the sales/marketing expertise of oleo chemicals. It sort of sounded of interest until Judy realised that the trio were not Disciples of Christ. Judy, most adamantly, neither envisaged nor wished to become partners with a company board of mixed beliefs. For her, "yoked together" was not going to be in any agreement, and we pulled the plug on further negotiations. This was most fortuitous as we later learnt that the Cognis senior managers would not have allowed any sale to proceed due to an undisclosed caveat that no insiders would be allowed to take over the manufacturing site. It was almost a touch of a secret agent from the woman of gold.

Sale of Richmond Property

Meanwhile, back at the ranch, whilst life was fully occupied working on finalising the Coolaroo purchase, there was also a full effort to achieve the maximum financial return from the sale of the Richmond site. This was realised by an offer from one of the divisions of the company that was undertaking the site valuation. Once Vicchem showed interest, the division then opened the possibility that we should leave the funds from the sale in the building of the new complex. The plan was that when this was completed, a higher return would become available. When told of this, Judy's response was immediate by grabbing me by my shirt lapels, shaking me like a wet rat, and stressing, "Remember, you have always quoted to me, 'The cobbler should stick to his last.' You know how to make chemicals but very little about property development. Stay with your last. Make and sell chemicals at Coolaroo!"

This advice was invaluable. The new Richmond complex took thirteen years before completion in late 2019. This was mainly caused by an obdurate Richmond Council balking at the building of 289 residences, including six townhouses; health clubs with ancillary equipment; three sky gardens with entertainment terraces, and three retail shops over thirteen floor levels on only 5,175 square metres of land.

Vicchem took the proffered cash for the Richmond land as recommended by Judy and sank it into Coolaroo. This presented 35,000 square metres of industrial land on which was a complete chemical factory built to German engineering standards, tank farms, laboratory, and warehouses. We then set out to do what we do well and make chemicals. Over the next sixteen years, sales increased by 250 per cent! Profitability followed in the wake.

Strangers at a Conference

As mentioned in paragraphs covering Judy's ministry at Open Air meetings of rounding up passing attendees, she was well known for her ability to make contact with strangers, wherever they might meet or under whatever conditions.

A typical example was at a conference in America. After the open breakfast, Judy and I separately circled to see who we might meet. A traditional way of telling whether a person could be open to a conversation is to see an individual wandering alone along the walls, wiling the time away, apparently studying paintings, scientific papers, or whatever can appear to be of interest.

Judy saw someone who fit the bill and sped over as an arrow to the bull's-eye. After some preliminaries, the conversation went something like this:

> Judy: And who do you work for?
>
> Fritz: Bayer, and who do you?
>
> Judy: Oh, you won't know us. It's Victorian Chemicals in Australia, but we do have a great product called HASTEN.
>
> Fritz: I know HASTEN. I've been in America for the last six months working with your product. It does work well.

And the rest, as they say, was history, and we visited Bayer Research Laboratories the next time we were in Germany.

When Business Gets Hard

When the Killick family finally bought Victorian Chemicals, it entered the world of capitalism with a capital C. We had entered an industry controlled by private owners (that's us) looking for profit. In the first instance Judy was not all that emotionally involved in the purchase to become a rich personage. It was simply after three months on the dole it would be a job for Bob and there would be something for the family to live on. The purchase of Victorian Chemicals showed her pragmatism. But she did add when talking with her close friend Marj, "If this doesn't work out, Marj, we may be living on your front lawn in a tent."

Weeks and months went by, and in the economic system, it felt like we were herding cats. Judy had wondered whether it was the Lord saying, "This is not My plan for you." But again, reviewing with friend Marj, Marj suggested, "I think we should encourage Bob to carry on because there would be nothing worse than to look back several years later and regret that we did not take up the opportunity."

During the scrappy negotiations and more wonderfully indeed through all the nooks and crannies of life together, Judy did "Stand by Me" as Tammy Wynette challenged her audiences sixty years ago.

Sometimes it's hard to be a woman
Given' all your love to just one man
You'll have the bad times
And he'll have the good times
Doing things that you don't understand

But if you love him, you'll forgive him
Even though he's hard to understand
And if you love him, oh, be proud of him
'Cause after all, he's just a man.

Judy was ahead of Tammy by following the Bible's words of Proverbs chapter 31, known as the hymn to a good wife, where verse 12 states, "All the days of her life, she does him good, not evil."

Is That a Profit?

Returning to capitalism and profit, Vicchem's early days were hard ones. The main problem was the long-inculcated company selling theme: "Don't look at the quality, look at the price." And with a low price, the profit margin was hard to find (sarcasm). After a couple of years, I returned home to impart that we had made a profit, and whilst I envisioned Judy's response would include many cheers and heavy spitting, Judy looked at the ledger and simply said, "But I don't see it."

The next day my first job was to be taught one of the key expressions of accountancy—source and application of funds, which provides an indication of the flow of cash through the business whilst the profitability/loss in any period, normally a month, can be obtained by summing the financial changes in the levels between months in debtors, stocks, creditors, and the level of money in the bank.

Judy found it preferable to keep to traditional Scottish financial wisdom:

> Never spend more than you earn, but that's easy as the Scots don't spend.
> The Scots never joke about money; it's too serious.
> Scots are not mean, they're canny.

Power Lady at a Meeting

Judy finds the following a little difficult to believe because it tells the difference in a meeting based on whether she is in attendance. When on the odd times I was travelling alone, the meeting tended to be relaxed. However, at the meetings Judy attended, as she walked in the door and, as I have already said, a lady not unattractive, the men smartened up. Let's start with pulling up your tie. It sounds mundane and trivial, but it happened.

Another time the meeting was among some of the semi-heavies of BASF. When Judy and I entered the room, there was a quite specific question from an attendee, who later turned out to be a smarty-pants who talked above his station. He asked, "What is that woman doing here?" with the sotto voice reply from one of his compatriots, "She owns the company." The tone of the meeting wonderfully changed.

Can a Joke Carry at a Business Meeting?

The story is set in the United States on the last day of school. Elections were held as to the pupils' futures. It was a unanimous vote that the school's dummkopf, fool, would be "The man most likely to be a failure in life."

Time passed, and at the twenty-fifth anniversary, who should turn up but the dummkopf in a chauffeured Rolls Royce, wife dripping with diamonds, the works. The flabbergasted former students wanted to know what had happened. "You were the dummkopf, you were the numskull, and you were the failure."

"I don't know," he replied. "I buy for $1; I sell for $3. That little margin seems to go such a long way! (With apologies to financiers.)

CHAPTER 9

Take Me Home, Oh, Muddah, Faddah, Take Me Home

Ne' ere be so humble, there's no place like home"
—From John Howard Payne's 1823 opera, *The Maid of Milan*

The younger son came to himself and said "I am about to starve, I will return to my father's house and say I have sinned ... treat me as one of your hired servants" ... The father responded—"This son of mine was dead but now he is alive" and so the feasting began!
—Luke 15:17–24

For those who need a time break with a trivia question, here it is. Which composer wrote an extremely classical piece of that became easy to parody? The parody can be easily heard on YouTube under "Camp Grenada Original Song" by Allan Sherman.

The composer was Amilcare Ponchielli, and the musical piece was known as the "Dance of the Hours" from his opera *La Gioconda.* It can be heard on YouTube under its traditional name and composer's photo.

The one thing the parody highlights is the overweening desire for someone to be home, which is reinforced by the other quotation: "There's no place like home." This chapter lingers around the effects that time provides differing aspects in a marriage rushing up to the length of sixty-four years.

Marriage Preparation

Most of the people of the world go through the same experience of living a single life and following a cultural ritual, living a married life.

The level of preparation varies from family to family, but preparation can come at two levels. The first is the wedding procedure itself, and the second is the preparation for the rest of one's life, which in Judy's case was going to last for sixty-four years and still adding. One attitude Judy has is that if you do anything, do it the best you can!

Feed the Boy

I suppose that if one is going to start preparation anywhere, the bride-to-be should start to think about how to feed the boy. Judy did not then know Napoleon's adage that "an army marches on its stomach," but she came to understand it. It would seem that the obvious way to appreciate what cooking was all about was to watch and learn from her mother as Freda prepared the family meals. This was where even the best ideas can stumble as Freda had a complete lack of interest in food preparation. Her heart was on the bowling greens, the tennis courts, the surf at Manly Beach, and a good game of canasta with the girls.

The standard evening meals were never fancy. Meat, when tabled, was based around sheep. Its low cost during Judy's teenage years (1950–1959) came from 100 to 120 million sheep in Australia against a population of 8.1 to 10 million people. The source of the meat came from lamb to mutton coming to the table as chops, shanks, casseroles (hot pot), any roast. Any leftovers returned as meat pancakes a couple of days later. If beef was to be on the table, sausages were it. Judy's brother, John, said his long-term remembrance of mealtimes was that tomato sauce always had a significant appearance on the table. If a light meal was considered, it was a toss-up between cheese on toast or fried rice.

Freda was not painted in the best light above, but for the right moments, she could produce her Pavlova as her pièce de résistance to be served as sliced party pieces or a dessert with ice cream. Considering that the main ingredients are six separated egg whites (60g), caster (superfine) sugar (270g), pure icing sugar (30g), and don't forget the 300 millilitres of whipped thickened cream, a real sugar kick has been produced. The Pavlova has a firm outer shell and a meringue texture inside. To provide the right taste experience, Freda would add a tartness by spreading the juice of a passion fruit on top of the cream layer. It had to be tasted to be believed. Judy followed well in her mother's steps.

Judy was not particularly enamoured with the thought of eating lamb variants for the rest of her life, as her mother, so her recipe book of 163 foolscap pages was commenced. It is a collection of recipes acquired from diverse sources such as women's magazines, newspapers, suggestions from friends, and prize-winning recipes of ladies who were pleased to have their names associated with their "special." The following ladies were some who made the cut:

> Apple Topping (Topsy); Bessie's Raspberry Shortcake; Beth's muffins; Beveridge Special; Doris's Apple Caramel; Dulcie's Sultana Cake; Fay's Ambrosia (Dessert); Ginger Slice, Millie Furlonger; Gwen's Burnt Butter Biscuits; Hazel's Bolognaise; Health Loaf (Joan); Jen's Brownies;

Joan's Slice; May's Lemon Meringue; Phil Richmond's Choc Logs; Quiche (Jenni's); Recipe of the month, Ruth Baker; Sheryl's Rice Salad; and Waterhouse-Sweet.

A typical page of the recipe book follows, although it is not quite typical as it is the actual page that contains the recipe for the pineapple fruitcake Judy made for Bob's honeymoon twenty-second birthday two days after their wedding.

Don't forget that first birthday cake.

Dress the Lady

Judy's natural abilities shone through the circumstances that her secondary school placement took her to a home science school as more fully discussed early in chapter 1. The elementary mathematics subject was flapdoodle, but Needlecraft and Garment Construction was a winner. Trigonometry was never going to be used again in her life whilst dressmaking became part of her life.

The queen of retro dressing.

The floral flock (*right*) was made going on forty years ago, is still worn, and has been appreciated by all who have seen it, even down to her granddaughter age's. Of interest was that a year ago, on ABC television, the lady newsreaders had become retro and were wearing a dress in the same style, black background, and large flowers.

This opens up the whole world of Judy's dress sense, which has been great!

This seamstress ability also gave Judy joy dressing up the children for fancy dress parties that still run to today.

Knitter

From her teenage years, Judy has also become a knitter learning mainly from her mother, who was good at plain, knit and purl styles. She later passed on her basic knowledge to daughter Jenni, who has been able to take it to a higher level with some classic cable and Fair Aisle patterns during those long early-morning hours in her days as an air traffic controller.

Clothing Longevity

Everybody seems to have their own buying habits and the clothing styles they prefer to wear. One of Judy's clothing characteristics is that she has a penchant for continuing to wear clothes irrespective of their style or age. This requires that the wearer's girth does not change over the years. Judy has followed this adage to the quarter centimetre. In the nautical vernacular, Judy's shape has been best summarised by W. S. Gilbert's description of a lovesick boy wooing his hoped-for intended, describing her:

For you are such a smart little craft,
Such a neat little, sweet little craft,
Such a bright little, tight little,
Slight little, light little,
Trim little, prim little craft!

Being lovesick really does make one speak in that way!

The most recent change in clothing started in the 1990s in what has become known as "fast fashion." During the last decade, there has been an inexorable increase in its market share. The first driving force was the speed from which haute-couture moved from catwalk to sophisticated retail outlets. During the same period, and from the other side of the counter, young women had more money to spend in their pockets. Lifestyle was important, and to be "in," a newly purchased garment was only worn once. That was indeed fast fashion. But it was never Judy-fashion. It was not that the goods were unavailable to her. Major players in Melbourne fast fashion are ZARA, H&M Group, and UNIQLO, and all three had boutique shops at Chadstone, "the fashion capital," which is but a seven-minute drive from home.

No Scottish lassie is ever going to wear a frock only once, not even just twice. Judy still wears some of her clothes for up to thirty to forty years. There is something uncanny about retro dressing.

Homemaking in the Middle Days

Many things happen during sixty-four years of homemaking, but the middle days are the period when family traditions and Judy's legacy are being concreted into the minds of the family's second generation and then to the grandchildren. It was the life Judy led where actions speak louder than words. The family have been inculcated by persistent exposure to three major aspects of life that make it worth living. These are *care* in all its elements, *fun* to enjoy life, and to apply the Latin carpe diem, to *seize the day.*

Care

Throughout her life, Judy has personified care in all its elements. This is a wide-sweeping statement since there are 213 synonyms and antonyms for "care" on Thesaurus.com and 917 synonyms and antonyms for "care for."

The strongest aspect of care is hospitality, which could be simply described as treating strangers and friends alike by welcoming them into our homes and lives.

Fun

The second is fun. This might be considered a quaint word to describe her life, but Judy's full personality exudes fun. The trouble is that the word itself gives it a sense of frippery that is not intended. We could read it was fun going to the movies, it was fun throwing a party, it was fun baking a cake, the comedian was fun. The word *fun* has become a cliché as a general description for having a good time. With much consideration, the family felt the best description is that Judy leads her life to the full, even when her cup is full and running over. It is the antithesis of many Christians who believe God was calling for a life of seriousness, even to eating lemons before they went out into the world.

Carpe Diem

The third is carpe diem, the innate skill of making most of the traits she has whenever an opportunity occurs—truly to seize the day! This is not to sound sophisticated for with Judy, it is just doing what comes naturally.

Might well have used Judy as the working model of the song "Doin' What Comes Naturally" from the operetta *Annie Get Your Gun* by Irving Berlin.

As Judy would go to the front door to meet arriving guests, her eyes, even her body, began to sparkle with the spirit of welcome.

Parenting

Judy's parental mission was to build a strong family. The inviolate rule was that there were to be no favourites. When there was a matter of import and the children were ageing, the whole family was to be involved in any discussions. During the deliberations, Judy and I never disagreed between ourselves in front of the children. The gatherings have matured into family council meetings, with the eldest now in their sixties with the youngest not running that far behind.

Another of her major projects was to develop the right approach to building a strong, growing family. The "right approach" has many definitions and for Judy, it comes back to what had been instilled in her during her early life. Her parents had married in November 1935, which was close enough to be right in the middle of the Great Depression. Judy remembers her father, before breakfast, perusing the *Sydney Morning Herald*'s birth reports from which he would organise his day's program of contacting the happy parents to sell them AMP Life Insurance for the newborn. First lesson: Work hard. His positive work ethic gave him early promotion from Orange to Newcastle. As an aside, this was not pleasing to Freda, who was pulled away from her lifetime friends.

The epitome was to handle money. Matters can go astray if money creeps in and causes family conflict. The key is that every generation must share equally without fear or contradiction.

The Clan of Children, Grandchildren, and Great-Grandchildren

So, we were married, and in the course of time, Judy and I had a daughter (Jenni) and two sons. In those days, the youngsters could travel on one of the parents' passports. This was Judy's documentation in 1969.

Passport travelling with Mum in 1969.
Peter, Jenny, Judy, and Andrew, left to right.

In the further course of time, each of these children married and had two children each. By 2023, our grandson had married and given us a great-grandson and great-granddaughter whilst our granddaughter had sired a great-granddaughter.

The clan came together to celebrate the forty-year anniversary of owning Victorian Chemicals.

And there we are. Bob and Judy have their first book, *As Good as Gold*, and Judy has her book, which you are now reading. Each of the clan has their own stories that they are developing at their own speeds and areas of expertise. We leave them to their successes and wait for the development of their life records.

Judy's Latter Years

These have been difficult for her.

Dementia

Our first major concern began on Friday night, December 19, 2014, when it became evident that Judy's eyes were playing-up. She commented during the washing and wiping up that she could see two faces of her grandson. The problem did not last for an extended time, and with it already past 9:30 p.m., it was agreed that we would leave matters until the morning.

There were no problems that next morning, but Jenni stressed that Judy should at least have a professional check her out. After much discussion, Jenni took Judy to an optometrist that afternoon who was available on the Corso. No problems were seen. Later that day, the Simpson grandchildren, Tim and Tara, joined the family at Camelot.

Sunday was a normal church Sunday at St Matthews. After tea and with no room at the card table, Judy used the dining room table for a quiet game of Patience. She broke up the big game, claiming that she couldn't remember how to play Patience, a game that she had played all her life. This was considered serious enough that at 8:30 p.m., the author drove Judy and Tara to the emergency section of Manly Hospital. From triage, she was immediately checked out, but again nothing was considered out of line. There was talk about going up to the North Shore Hospital, but it was soon negated as too far and too much bother.

The next three days—Monday, Tuesday, and Wednesday—life returned to the Manly holiday mood with no problem sighted. The holiday culminated on Thursday with a very happy 2014 Christmas lunch starting at 12:30 p.m. and finishing at around 4:30 p.m. We then prepared to return to Melbourne.

The trip home had us staying in Canberra with the Simpsons Friday and Saturday nights, journeying home down the Hume Highway on Sunday. Our first chance to book an MRI appointment was 2:45 p.m. for Tuesday, January 30. It was then confirmed that Judy had damaged brain tissue from a stroke/brain haemorrhage.

We have been in our own modified lives for the last ten years of mind-block versus remembering-all, definitely a difficult time for one and all of us.

Osteoporosis

If December 19, 2014, was a date noted for dementia, then June 27, 2021, would be elected for the arrival of the impact of osteoporosis. Judy had weeded the garden most of the latter Sunday afternoon and was getting ready for bed when back pain hit her with a vengeance. She was unable to move and ended up kneeling at her bedside with her head on the mattress. Fortunately, at the earliest mention of the pain, a paracetamol tablet had been given to her, and after an hour, she had enough relief to lie flat on the bed overnight.

For the next four months, Judy bounced between a chiropractor, a physiotherapist, and our doctor. The latter two finally agreed that we should get her to Waverley Hospital for a CT scan. The next day, October 29, spinal crushed fractures were confirmed with the best medical advice being to rest. This was the last advice Judy wanted to hear and/or take. Judy has reasonably endured the three years that have gone by since the osteoporosis diagnosis. The main symptom for osteoporosis is back pain caused by a collapsed bone in the spine. A related sign is a bone that breaks much more easily than expected. For Judy, this occurred two and a half months later with a clean break of a metatarsal in her foot. She finds it necessary to consume eight tablets a day to manage pain control at the time of writing. Whilst this chapter heading is "Five Foot Two," a symptom of the disease predicts a loss of height over time, and she is now four foot eight. This also relates to a stooped posture, another sign of osteoporosis.

Bacterial Infection

On the February 19, 2023, Judy had the double whammy of osteoporosis pain and a bacterial infection. An ambulance needed to be called and a bed found for her in Monash Public Hospital. There she was for the next eleven days, which is not an insignificant time. Judy spent the long nights continuing to call out for Bob. During a visit one day, one of the nurses cottoned on to who I was and said, "So you're Bob!" Such is a reputational build-up. Judy was discharged at 10 a.m. on March 1.

These were the three significant sicknesses that have put Judy through a wringer. But she has carried on.

CHAPTER 10

Among the Gold

Gold there is, and rubies in abundance, but lips that speak knowledge are a rare jewel.

—Proverbs 20:15

A good name is more desirable than great riches; to be esteemed is better than silver or gold.

—Proverbs 22:1

True adornments aren't available in department stores nor can they be bought in a beauty shop.

—Anonymous

After our earlier publication of *As Good as Gold,* the request came for a biography about Judy. To the idea, Judy provided a touch of modified hysteria mainly on the basis that there was nothing to write about. Judy ultimately agreed, claiming that "Well, there is no harm in giving it a go. Anyway, the book will be all over in fifty pages."

Very early in the process, the potential title *A Woman of Gold* came to our minds. The immediate challenge was whether this was an appropriate title as it revolved around the word "gold," which will always be personally interpreted by every individual who reads it in his or her context.

Dangers: There Is Gold

Greed—King Midas of Phrygia

The story of Midas has lasted over two thousand years with its teaching on the dangers of greed. Midas, having gotten on the good side of the mythical god Dionysus, was promised that he would be granted any wish he had. He asked for, and received, the power that all he touched would turn to gold. Midas soon found that his choice was an extremely bad call. He found himself starving although his golden food at each meal was telling him how much wealthier he was becoming. The end of the line came when Midas inadvertently touched his beautiful only daughter.

Greed—Golden Goose

The story tells of a farmer and his wife who found that in their gaggle of geese was one that would lay a golden egg each day. After several months, their minds lingered on greed and reasoned that they could realise all the gold that was awaiting them in the goose. That very night they killed the bird and found no gold in the carcase. And now, nor was there a live goose that would continue to provide a slow but steady golden-egg-income.

Idolatry

The Bible lays down the law. Actually, it is the Tenth Commandment:

> Don't set your hearts on anything that is your neighbour's. (Ex. 20:17 MSG)

And in the New Testament:

> Put to death whatever belongs to your earthly nature … and greed, which is idolatry? (Col. 3:5)

Pride

> When you eat and are satisfied; when you build fine houses and settle down; when your herds and flocks grow large; when your silver and gold increase; and all you have is multiplied, then your heart will become proud and you will forget the Lord your God! (Deuteronomy 8:12–13)

Lust for Gold

> But if it's only gold these leaders are after, they'll self-destruct in no time. Lust for money brings trouble and nothing but trouble. (1 Timothy 6:9–10 MSG)

Love for Money

> Princess Leia Organa: It's not over yet.
>
> Han Solo: It is for me, sister. Look, I ain't in this for your revolution, and I'm not in it for you, Princess. I expect to be well paid. I'm in it for the money.
>
> Princess Leia Organa: You needn't worry about your reward. If money is all that you love, then that is what you will receive.

There Is Gold! A Country Interlude

Welcome to the Great Australian Gold Rush

It needs to be remembered that the one thing that gold provides is impact, even on a country, no matter how large or small. The miners individually catch gold fever that spawns a group contagious excitement, which becomes an unstoppable, insatiable gold rush. The best photo to provide an understanding of the fever is from the 1896 Klondike Gold Rush in the Yukon, Alaska, showing the unending stream of miners on their way up and over the hills on their way to the digging fields.

The Golden Staircase of Chilkoot Pass to the Yukon.

For Australia, the starter's gun had been fired on May 15, 1851, when the newspapers published Hargreaves' discovery of gold at Ophir, near Orange, NSW. Within one week, three hundred miners were digging in the locality, a true presage of what was to come. At this time, the country was a lawless prison colony of England, but within the twenty years, to 1871, Australia's population quadrupled from 430,000 to 1,700,000 people. And by 1901, fifty years from the original article, there went the prison colony and in came the fledgling nation of Australia. The 1901 Federation Census recorded the country's population of 3,773,801 souls in a country that had become multinationalised and multiculturised to a classless, wealthy, liberal society that was the envy of the world. It had established parliamentary elections that were by secret ballot, the workers' eight-hour day, and a fully established Labour Party to guard workers' rights. The demonstration of its vibrant economy was evidenced by the way minor docks, such as Melbourne, had become major international ports from which Australia exported more goods than it imported.

The gold rush insatiably sucked in newcomers from all over the world. Its drawing power lay in Australia's land size with gold finds occurring in one state after another. The diggings were prosperous; there were gold nuggets just under the surface. Such was the case of The Welcome Stranger, the largest nugget ever discovered in the world and which weighed in at a gross seventy-eight kilograms from which seventy-one kilograms of gold were obtained. It was found three centimetres under the surface of the now ghost town of Moliacul (60 kilometres west of Bendigo) in 1869. The second-largest is The Welcome Nugget, which was discovered eleven years earlier at Bakery Hill, Ballarat, and weighed sixty-nine kilograms.

Like any statement, it is open for discussion, but it can be easily claimed that the gold rush was Australia's golden ball of opportunity. And more important, the people grabbed it with both hands. It would seem that gold did not just provide wealth but entered the psyche of the nation. Looking back, there had been the great blend, or "The Mix," throughout the country between the convicts and the free settlers. The saving grace was the answer to "How criminal were the convicts?" or, "How criminal was it to steal washing off a clothesline?" The challenge goes back to *The Mikado,* Gilbert and Sullivan's comic opera set in Japan, in which it is stated, "My object all sublime, I shall achieve in time, to make the punishment fit the crime, the punishment fit the crime!" The answer back in the late 1700s to the 1800s was a free trip to the antipodes at His Majesty's expense with beachfront accommodation and organic food on the menu! It was not the nobles but the poor who came, the convicts under the duress of poverty, the free settlers fleeing poverty. Poverty had each group understanding each other so as the gold accumulated, it worked through the country's psyche starting with the little Aussie battler," moving to the "Aussie spirit of mateship," and the Aussie who was always ready to have a go!

Eureka Stockade

The Mix also produced an antigovernment spirit. This, not unexpectedly, started in the goldfields over the issues of the cost of a miner's licence and unfair laws that made them unable to claim the land on which they worked. These and some other issues had been simmering, but finally, Australian's only revolution boiled over on Sunday, December 3, 1854, in the Eureka gold diggings of Ballarat. The miners built a palisade, and the event was labelled "The Eureka Stockade." The miners were not very practiced at revolting, and the whole rebellion was over on the first day! "We were outgunned," said the diggers.

In the meantime, the government had decided to make an example of the eleven ringleaders it had in jail. There were great preparations for the trial, which was to run from February 22 to March 27, 1855. It was held in the Victorian Supreme Court in Melbourne with Chief Justice Sir William a'Beckett, presiding and the prosecution in the hands of the attorney general, Mr W. F. Stawell, and the solicitor-general, Mr Molesworth. The charge was high treason set forth in ominous detail. The first paragraph of the indictment read:

> The charge is that you did on the 3rd December, 1854, being then in warlike manner, traitorously assemble together against our Lady the Queen, and that you did, whilst so armed and assembled together levy and make war against our said Lady the Queen within part of her dominions called Victoria, and attempt by force of arms to destroy the Government constituted there and by law established, and to depose our Lady the Queen from the kingly name and her Imperial Crown.

It was soon recognised that there was mass public support for the fossickers. No record can determine who provided the legal funds, but the prisoners soon found they had on their side the most eminent fighting counsel of the period in Messrs. Ireland, Aspinall, Michie, Cope, and Dawson. The first prisoner before the court was Timothy Hayes.

After the trial was over, the newspapers agreed that it had been a fiasco. It all fell over in that no witnesses could agree. To put it in the vernacular, neither the police nor the army nor the rebels were the sharpest tools in the shed, and all became entangled in the cross-examinations. After the closing arguments, the jury deliberated for thirty minutes before the not guilty verdict was announced to a sudden burst of applause in the court and the ten thousand observers in the streets. The chief justice could see the flow of the tide and left the rest of the trials to a lower-court judge. It was a useless farce since there was never any hope of a conviction. Counsel wandered off into other courts to attend to more profitable business and had to be called in to criticise evidence they had not heard. They were perfectly candid in assuring the Crown that there was no chance of a conviction. They knew they could rely on the jury.

The Ballarat rioters were all formerly acquitted on April Fool's Day 1855, and that really says it all!

Lasseter's Lost Reef

A classic example of the Aussie psyche is the mythic story of Harold Bill Lasseter and his claim to have found a fabulously rich gold deposit in a remote and desolate corner of Central Australia. The reef has never been located again. On his last expedition, he fell out with Paul Johns, his travelling companion, his two remaining camels bolted, and weakened and blinded, he died of malnutrition and exhaustion. His emaciated body was found in 1931 at Winters Glen. The last prospecting expedition to find Lasseter's Reef was undertaken by his elderly son, Bob Lasseter, in 2013 without success. The last public reference to it was in 2017 with an episode *Lasseter's Gold: Expedition Unknown* on the American Travel Channel in which the mystery was examined. The story of Lasseter and his reef is slowly fading from the minds of the millennial generation, but it remains well-fixed among the older ones.

Five of Judy's antecedents were not unaffected by gold fever in the rush. They were all-in with bells on.

Grandfather Frederick McFadzean had led a normal life until the family moved from Melbourne to Orange in NSW. Big changes happened for him in the early 1920s when, after leaving Robert Harper and Sons selling food additives, he had positions of shareholder, manager, and managing director of eleven mining companies over ten years. The local newspapers reported Fred as a super-optimist (1925) and walking down the streets of Orange with £300 of gold in his pockets (1931). Further details are recorded in chapter 6.

Judy's great-grandfather, Mathew McFadzean, has been that true hidden black sheep antecedent. His birth, death, and marriage are established by certificates, but that is it. When and where he arrived in Australia has not been ascertained; indeed, there is no mention of him in any third-party documentation. The one snippet that puts him near a goldfield is his occupation on his marriage certificate, which states "Minerals Speculator."

Gold brought secondary economies, and when it was discovered at Cadia on the other side of Mount Conobolas from Orange, Judy's grandfather set up an outpost of his Orange mercer's business. Nothing else is known of entrepreneurial spirit except that in 1921 a fire burned the buildings to the ground, and there was no further mention.

Louis Kitz, Judy's great-great-grandfather came to Australia with his family in 1853, settling in Geelong. With an entrepreneurial spirit, "he was in everything but a bath," commencing with watchmaking and clock making, jewellery, wine merchant, and cider manufacturer. He went on to be the first importer of a quartz crushing machine, which he soon had working at the Steigleitz diggings halfway between Geelong and Bendigo with good success.

And both lastly and quite tenuously, there were William Mower Akhurst, showman extraordinaire and his wife, Ella, the actress, not forgetting them as Judy's great-great-great-grandparents. The family had arrived in Adelaide from Scotland in 1849, and from there, in 1854 had moved on to Melbourne, Victoria, which was then known as The Golden Colony. They were where the crowds were, the money was, and their activities blossomed. They had thirteen children, so it is doubtful how much time Ella had left for the stage. Another truth that rapidly became apparent was that most miners never made money mining for gold. The money went to the service providers.

Blessings: There Is Gold

A Gift from God

You may say to yourself, "My power and the strength of my hands have produced this wealth for me." But remember the Lord your God, for it is He who gives you the ability to produce wealth (Deut. 8:17–18).

The blessing of the Lord brings wealth (Prov. 10:22).

The foundation is Jesus Christ Himself, and when anyone builds a life on that foundation—whether the materials are gold, silver, precious stones, wood, hay, or stubble—it will be shown for what it is by fire (1 Cor. 3:12–14 free translation). Moral: Build your life by acquiring biblical knowledge, wisdom, and faith (Prov. 16:16 et al.).

Now that we have skirted around the edges, at least, of the different impacts gold can have on humanity, for the rest of the chapter, it is appropriate to consider one person in a provocative statement.

Judith Helen Killick, a Woman of Gold

During her Christian life, Judy has been a God-fearer.

"You're kidding," do I hear you say? Not really for, as it was claimed earlier, all understandings come back to definitions. The trouble lies in that when a God-fearer is mentioned, most people expect to greet a sour-faced, sullen, bad-tempered person who ate five lemons before entering the room. A real God-fearer is *not* someone who says to people they meet, "I am a worm. Tread on me!" Indeed, to change the metaphor, you will get the feeling when you are near Judy that you are in the presence of a sleek racing car with the delightful sound of the engine purring under the bonnet indicating her strong working relationship with her God and who has God's Spirit, which provides the driving force through life.

The most important distinction to know whether you have met a God-fearer is to be careful what you consider. When the prophet Samuel was looking for the first King of Israel, God had to speak to him: "Looks aren't everything. Don't be impressed with looks and stature. I've already eliminated him. God judges persons differently than humans do. Men and women look at the face; God looks into the heart" (1 Sam. 16:7 MSG).

The New Testament follows the same theme in 1 Timothy 2:9–10 (MSG): "I want ladies to get into humility before God, not primping before a mirror, or chasing the latest fashions, or adornments of gold and precious stones but doing something beautiful for God and becoming beautiful in doing it!"

The following observations of Judy can be made as she grew over the years as a true God-fearer:

Her Direct Relationship with God

Judy has reverence, even awe, even fear of God. She recognises that God is for her and has faith that Jesus can do anything. And she is available and willing to be used by Him, is always open and prepared for God's plans, and summarily to walk in love and obedience with the Almighty.

From Wife to Mother to Matriarch

This fits in with her husband's plans with two talking and walking as one; maintains a witness for God whilst passing on her faith in and through the family; works hard to take care of the home, endeavouring that appropriate snatches of Proverbs 31 happen in the day-to-day housework.

Ministry in the Local Church

Faithfully attends church on Sunday unless away from home; participates in every ministry opportunity; is faithful in supporting other believers practically and fiscally. She helps younger women into godliness with others to become witnesses for Christ. Her work is supported and acknowledged by other believers.

In Society

Lives honourably and wisely; does not gossip or speak ill of others. She is financially responsible and gives generously to those in need. She tells others what Jesus has done for her and demonstrates care and love.

Her Inner Life

Judy sparkles in the company of people and behaves naturally. She studies the teachings of Jesus, strives for holiness and kindness, lives out her faith for Him, and stands firm in the faith.

At the beginning of chapter 4, one of Judy's close friends provided us with a word portrait of Judy to provide some background for those who might never have met her. As the book is starting to slowly draw to a close, another close friend, Mrs Elaine Oliver, a former legal secretary and of late a key Bible teacher in Bible Study Fellowship (BSF), has provided diverse angles that can provide the reader with remembrances of what has been read:

Sometimes you meet a Christian woman who you think you would like to learn from and maybe emulate one or two godly characteristics you see in her. Rarely do you have the opportunity to get close to someone who has several such characteristics, and you realise God has brought this person into your life, not just for good company and friendship, but for you to learn from. Judy is such a woman.

> From her gracious hospitality to many; her never-tiring efforts to share Jesus with whoever she meets; her generous, loving, and kind spirit; her steadfast prayer life; the way she joyfully and encouragingly visits many people; her happy, thoughtful, caring, and prayerful phone calls; her love of her husband and family and keen interest in their lives; her everyday living, not self-indulging but desiring to be wise with what God has given her.

Truly, "I thank God every time I remember you." (Phil. 1:3).

"The righteous … will still bear fruit in old
age, they will stay fresh and green."
(Ps. 92:14)

A Final, Final Summary

As a woman of gold, Judy looks back on her eighty-four years of life
and delights to repeat Paul's statement of faith:

For whatsoever has happened to me,
Has happened for the furtherance of the gospel. (Phil. 1:12)

Thank you for reading Judy's life story,
A Woman of Gold, yet a servant.

HELPFUL AND HOPEFUL ILLUMINATIONS OF THE ILLUSTRATIONS

Bob Killick and Wendy Miles

Chapter 1 - Five Foot Two, Eyes of Blue

1939 On the Washing Basket. Judy's birth year.

Old-Fashioned Washing Line. Reminds us of the line of life.

The Grass. Tells us we are all still of the earth, earthy.

Yabbie Hanging Off the Bathers. Judy's lifetime swimming prowess at Manly Beach.

Prefect/Perfect Towel. She was a school prefect and Bob's "perfect."

Tennis Rackets. Judy has loved tennis all her life.

Stylish Tennis Dress. Her sporting attitude to her life and her femininity.

Boxer Shorts. Bob.

Tea Towels. Judy relishes her role as the washer of the dishes, happy in the life of a servant.

The Gold Pans. Symbolic of things to come in both natural and supernatural realms. Judy's intuitive modus operandi has been the infusion of her faith in all things, "sifting for gold."

Music Notes. Her lifetime love of music, singing, and song.

Quick March. Judy's change from shy girl to affirmative woman days as a prefect who directed a school and grew an attachment to, and ease with, the microphone. "Give me a microphone, and I'll emote." Her ability to ad lib and excel in the art of improvisation were depended upon by her producer, Bob.

Jeans on the Clothesline. The unfolding blessings of the family genes over the years.

Jeans Hung Last. Because it can take a lifetime to see the gifts and abilities, strengths and even weaknesses bestowed upon us via our hereditary lineage.

"It will all come out in the wash." Tells us to let God have His slow unfolding through our lives.

Chapter 2 - We've Travelled Along, Singing Our Song, Side by Side

Jesus Folk. Name of the first musical undertaken by Syndal Baptist Church of which Judy was the Jesus folk leader.

Gospel Theatre. The theatre troupe that evolved at Syndal Baptist Church using three musicals written by the Salvation Army Englishmen Gowans and Larsson.

Singing Christmas Tree. Our church's Christmas *pièce de résistance* for five years and unique to Australia with 250 participants trained by a lady from First Dallas Baptist Church, in the United States.

Picnic Rug and Contents. Judy's voluntary "sustenance to those in need before showtime."

Mice. The plague witnessed whilst performing at Rainbow/Hopetoun in Western Victoria.

Judy Centre Stage with the Tambourine. As always with her familiar high kick of the leg.

"**He came to give us life!"** The life force that eventuated from the musicals.

Hallelujah!. The well of joy that accompanied the Gospel Theatre whenever they were on the road with the accompanying cry, "It's showtime!"

Chapter 3 - Wives Were Made to Love and Kiss

"It Was Meant." Judy would often use this phrase. In 1960, it was her marriage.

"Husband Material" List. Only one item that counts, faith.

Rainbow. The promises made in marriage and God's promises to us.

Judy at Her Desk, Typing. Throughout the decades—school, speed typist at Bank of Wales, speed typist for Bob (223-page PhD thesis, "Aza Steroids and Steroids"), Vicchem Company Books, Bob's book *As Good As Gold.*

Bells, Books, Clock, and "Quick." Indicate the pressure of deadlines on Judy.

A "Typeical" Day. "Type-ical" is a play on "always typing," converting to a "typical day."

Couple in the Garden. Understanding Eden.

The Non-Linear Path. The twists and turns of life, the non-linear nature of our Christian walk.

Face in the cloud. The heavens smiling over us.

Tempus Fugit. Latin for "time flies." Sixty-four years of marriage passed so quickly.

Angel Tent. The biblical truth that angels encamp about the dwellings of the just to guard and protect us.

Chapter 4 - Ain't She Sweet?

The Stage of Life. Judy's love of it and joy in performing.

It's showtime. A genetic trail witnessed throughout the matriarchal line.

Freda. Judy's mum, who loved the stage so much and was performing at ten years of age.

"**Script Unknown.**" Refers to both human and spirit realms. "For you do not know what a day brings forth," and the necessity to ad lib/improvise in concerts over the years.

Hearts. The motivation underpinning all Judy did on the stage, including the heart of the gospel.

Dinky Judy's much-loved family dog.

Vase of flowers. Judy's love of roses.

Ellen Tully. The actress, from an artistic family, married William Mower Akhurst ('Mower') and brought show business genes into the family, thirteen babies notwithstanding.

Mower. The great-great-grandfather of Judy, a writer and producer.

Alice Akhurst. Judy's grandmother, Freda's mother, known for her parties and hospitality.

Bob the Producer. Someone has to pull the show together.

Chapter 5 - Scotland the Brave

The Ship. The *Midlothian* that brought the Gillies to Australia from Scotland.

c. 1837. The year it departed Scotland (August) and entered Sydney Heads (December).

129 days. Length of their journey.

"Forever." "Farewell and good riddance." The occupants fled poverty in search of a better life.

Land Ahoy. Land is what the immigrants sought.

Cherry Blossom. Attendance at the annual Cherry Blossom Parade, Main Street, Orange, NSW, featured throughout Judy's childhood.

Immigrants' Vicissitudes. The relentless cycle of drought, flood, fire, bushranger attacks, and then a bumper crop beset by a price crash from oversupply.

Land of the Brave. For the above reasons and possibly more.

Land of Beachfronts. What they longed for and hoped they would get but perhaps did not.

Gillies Tailor, Outfitter in Orange. - J. Gillies (Judy's grandfather) in 1892 purchased a clothier, tailor, mercer, and outfitter business in Orange.

Judy with her hands on her head. Such a lot of history in the hope of beachfront property!

Chapter 6 - My 'Ain Folk

First Quartz Crusher. Released the gold from the ore.

The Pile of Gold Pans. The perpetual looking for gold over the generations.

Gold scales "still zero." Finding hardly anything and definitely not the mother lode.

Lucknow Co. Not too much luck though. Eleven companies set up and liquidated. The year the last two were liquidated, Judy was born.

The Golden Days. The banner over Judy's bloodline who hoped/dreamt of finding gold. The fortitude, the persistence, the fun, passions (politics), and heartache along the way.

Woman pointing to gold pan dishes. Judy not seeking but spotting potential gold in Vicchem through patents.

Party flags, Japanese lanterns. All signify the jolliest parties of the week held by Freda.

The tennis court. - At Judy's grandparents' home, Hine Taimoa. Countless games of tennis were played, attracting some of the greats in Australian tennis. It's also symbolic of the large entertaining room at the rear of the house referred to as "The Court," where many parties were held. It was the place to be.

"Go Daphne." Daphne Akhurst, Judy's mother's cousin, was the famous tennis star of the 1920s who also played there. The Australian Ladies Tennis Singles Annual Championship is named after her.

Chapter 7 - When the Saints Go Marching In

A Simple Illustration. Signifies the accessibility and simplicity of entering the kingdom of God.

Friends. Judy's lifelong attempt to gather friends, family, neighbours, church, community.

Arms Up. Reflects a tilt of the heart heavenward, an action, a position of humility and grace.

Oh Bountiful. Where beauty and abundance are.

Butterflies. A simple analogy of what it's like to be born again. An experience of a spiritual awakening, beauty personified. A butterfly is sensitive to the breeze if it wishes to fly as Christians are to the wind of the Spirit of God.

Cocoons. The old you is left behind as you emerge anew.

Tree. Full to the brim, beautiful, representing an abundant life.

Chapter 8 - She's the Girl who Broke the (Casino) Bank at Monte Carlo

Pencils. Deep down, Judy often wondered what she was signing, but pencils do have rubbers!

Oh!? Director of the Victorian Chemical Company Proprietary Limited in 1983 with no previous experience. One can only trust the united family.

Chocolate Chips Ahoy! Not just a pretty face but an out-of-the-box thinker. Symbolised by three historic inventions in one (biscuits, 1588; chocolate bars, 1847; and chocolate chip biscuits, 1930).

Stay with Your Cast Iron Last. Judy believed the motto "Stick to what you're good at."

Opportunity Knocks. And so agreed to go with Bob, but may end up living in a tent.

HASTEN. Judy's social skills and right word, right time result in the addition of Germany.

Who's That Woman? Wrong question for a male to ask about a female in the boardroom!

Plumes. Judy's quiet yet flamboyant confidence and spark make everything shine.

Crown. An excellent wife is the crown of her husband.

$1, $3. Shareholdings that multiply year on year until they're worth millions!

Chapter 9 - Take Me Home, Oh, Muddah, Faddah, Take Me Home

Board Meeting. The reality of family business meetings over breakfast. Yes, even the bank manager attended.

What Fun! Fun was compulsory at work/home, and there was always a joke.

Authentic Frippery. Authentic fun rather than showy.

The Family Council. Held more like a board meeting to be fair to all. Certain codes held such as everyone gets equal returns from the company.

Recipe Books. Imagine 163 foolscap pages of her favourite recipes on the table.

Patterns. Her lifelong love of dressmaking. Perhaps patterns begot patents?

Construction in the Middle Years. How Judy crafted success in the middle years from needlecraft and construction through to homemaking, hospitality. and business.

Hang onto Things You Love for a Very Long Time. Judy's modus operandi in everything, including her clothes. She still wears a dress she made forty years ago for formal occasions.

Knit to Land Well. Like Mother, like daughter, Jenny's industriousness on night shift leads to knitting between the rare landing of planes in the air traffic control tower at Adelaide Airport.

Chapter 10 - Among the Gold

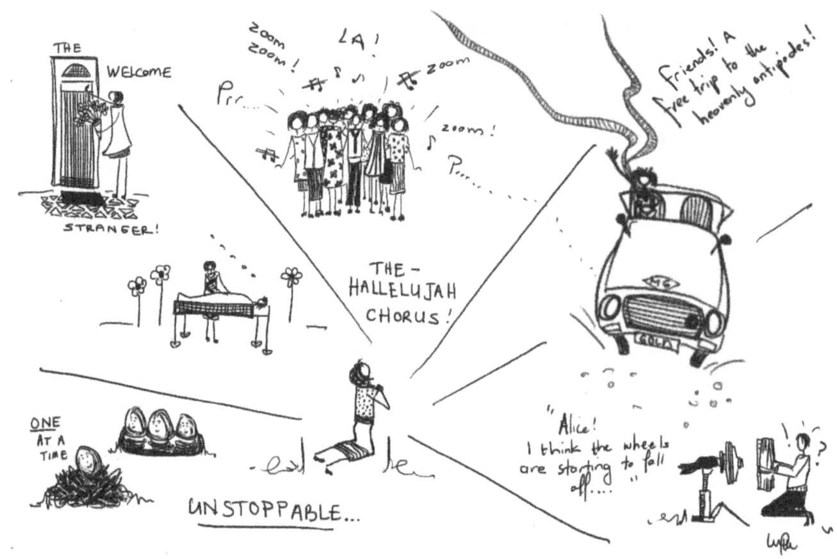

The Golden Goose. Only lays one golden egg each day.

The Welcome Stranger. Name given to the largest gold nugget ever discovered in the world. Here it also speaks of Judy's willingness and joy in reaching out to others, knocking on the doors of strangers and welcoming them to the neighbourhood or to church.

Woman Praying. Prayer is central in Judy's life, particularly for the sick.

The Hallelujah Chorus. Judy was ever thankful, rejoicing always.

Zoom! La! Judy and the Gospel Theatre's exuberance and love of life.

The Choir. Judy's lifelong joy in music and song and community.

Purring. The sound of a sleek racing car, likened to Judy's relationship with her God.

MG. The sleek racing car taking Judy and whoever she persuades to the heavenly antipodes.

Broken Wheel. The slow impact of osteoporosis, the cardiovascular event(s), and dementia.

The Rays of Light. Ever exuding from the woman of gold, yet a servant.

'So, is that the last Peg Bob?!'

POSTSCRIPT

As the final Edit had just returned from the publisher and we had started working through the last checking, Judy was "Promoted to Glory."

For some months we had heard her say that her life was over and her only desire was to go and meet with her Lord. On the Saturday morning of the 13th April 2024, and after not sleeping all Friday night, she reported that "I'm not feeling well and I want to go to Heaven." Judy then dozed off and on but fell heavily mid-afternoon walking in the kitchen.

After 3 hours at the hospital the Senior Nurse suggested I talk to her and hold her hand as she was slipping away into our Lord's presence. Now, free from suffering, she awaits that glorious day of resurrection.

When we all get together –
What a day of rejoicing that will be.